Bold Women
in
California History

KAY
MOORE

Bold Women in California History

KAY MOORE

2017
Mountain Press Publishing Company
Missoula, Montana

Cover art © 2017 Stephanie Frostad
Sketches on pages iii and 4 by Stephanie Frostad
Maps on pages vi and x by Chelsea Feeney

Library of Congress Cataloging-in-Publication Data

Names: Moore, Kay, 1950- author.
Title: Bold women in California history / Kay Moore.
Description: Missoula, Montana : Mountain Press Publishing Company, 2017. |
 Series: Bold women series
Identifiers: LCCN 2017030423 | ISBN 9780878426799 (pbk. : alk. paper)
Subjects: LCSH: Women—California—Biography. | Women—California—History. |
 California—Biography.
Classification: LCC CT3262.C25 M66 2017 | DDC 920.0794—dc23
LC record available at https://lccn.loc.gov/2017030423

MP Mountain Press
PUBLISHING COMPANY
P.O. Box 2399 • Missoula, MT 59806 • 406-728-1900
800-234-5308 • info@mtnpress.com
www.mountain-press.com

To the many wonderful women I met in California who continue to influence the state with their fortitude and dreams

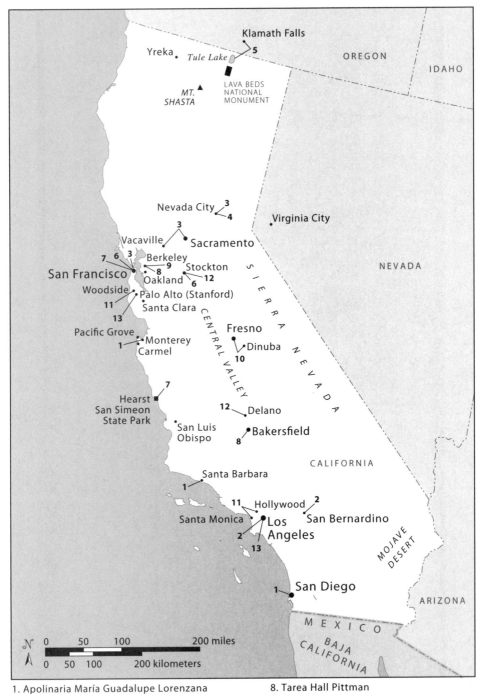

Klamath Falls
Yreka · · **5**
Tule Lake
OREGON
IDAHO
LAVA BEDS
NATIONAL
MONUMENT
▲
MT.
SHASTA

Nevada City **3**
4
Virginia City
NEVADA

3
Vacaville Sacramento
7 **6** **3** Berkeley
San Francisco **8** **9** Stockton
Oakland **6** **12**
Woodside Palo Alto (Stanford)
11
13 Santa Clara
Pacific Grove Fresno
1 Monterey · Dinuba
Carmel **10**

CENTRAL VALLEY
SIERRA NEVADA

7
Hearst
San Simeon
State Park
12 Delano
San Luis
Obispo Bakersfield
8

CALIFORNIA

Santa Barbara
1
11 Hollywood **2**
Santa Monica Los San Bernardino
2 Angeles
13
MOJAVE
DESERT

1 San Diego
ARIZONA
M E X I C O
BAJA
CALIFORNIA

N
0   50   100   200 miles
0 50 100   200 kilometers

1. Apolinaria María Guadalupe Lorenzana
2. Bridget "Biddy" Mason
3. Luzena Stanley Hunt Wilson
4. Nellie Elizabeth Pooler Chapman
5. Toby "Winema" Riddle
6. Elvira Virginia Mugarrieta
7. Julia Morgan

8. Tarea Hall Pittman
9. Yoshiko Uchida
10. Rose Ann Vuich
11. Shirley Temple Black
12. Dolores Huerta
13. Sally Ride

Contents

Acknowledgments

Sometimes historical research leads one to more questions than answers. My deepest thanks to the following people who kindly responded to my queries and tried to help me find the answers:

Charla Wilson, Collections Manager, Women's Museum of California, San Diego; Lesli MacNeil, Assistant, Alumnae Association, Mills College, Oakland; Janice Braun, Library, Mills College, Oakland; Marilou Ficklin, Doris Foley Library for Historical Research, Nevada City; Richard Dennison, sector superintendent of California State Parks Old Town San Diego in collaboration with park staff members Ellen Sweet and Linda Jacobo; Dr. Paula J. Birnbaum, Associate Professor, Department of Art + Architecture, University of San Francisco; Carl Mautz of Carl Mautz Publishing; Rosemarie Mossinger, book designer; Pat Chesnut, director, Searls Historical Library, Nevada City, CA; Gretchen Louden, reference section, Stockton–San Joaquin County Public Library, Stockton; Scott Cornett, Tulare County ag commissioner's office; Dr. Katy Anderson, Steven Dunn, and the other members of the Tuesday Painters group; Lynda Griblin and granddaughter Lucy; Tricia Gesner of the Associated Press; the staff at Rancho Los Coches RV Park; Lorna Kirwan, Michael Maire Lange, and Jennie Hinchcliff at the Bancroft Library at UC Berkeley; Laura Sorvetti, Special Collections and Archives, Robert E. Kennedy Library, Cal Poly, San Luis Obispo; and special thanks to Jennifer Carey, who accepted the challenge to act as my editor on top of an already established workload. My love and thanks to Bryan and Kristina Moore, who always support my writing efforts, and also then two-year-old Hailey, who learned the word "mystery" from listening to Gran'ma Kay talk about her writing issues and promised to help her find a solution!

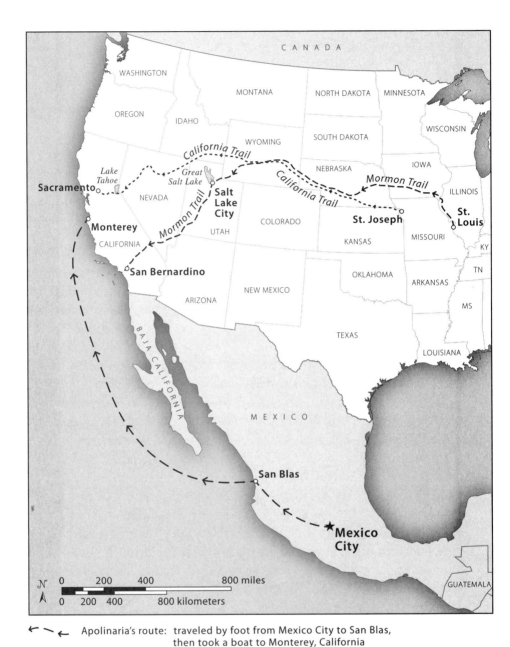

CANADA

WASHINGTON

MONTANA   NORTH DAKOTA   MINNESOTA

OREGON
                IDAHO   WISCONSIN

                        WYOMING   SOUTH DAKOTA

California Trail   IOWA

Lake
Tahoe   Great   NEBRASKA   Mormon Trail   ILLINOIS
Sacramento   Salt Lake   California Trail

        NEVADA   Salt
                  Lake
                  City   COLORADO   St.
Monterey   St. Joseph   Louis
        UTAH   MISSOURI
CALIFORNIA   KY
                                        KANSAS
        San Bernardino   TN

                        NEW MEXICO   OKLAHOMA   ARKANSAS

            ARIZONA   MS

BAJA CALIFORNIA   TEXAS

                                              LOUISIANA

        MEXICO

        San Blas

                    Mexico
                    City
                                              GUATEMALA

N
0   200   400   800 miles
0   200   400   800 kilometers

← ~ ←   Apolinaria's route: traveled by foot from Mexico City to San Blas,
                              then took a boat to Monterey, California

←－－← Biddy's route: walked the Mormon Trail from St. Louis, Missouri, through
                              Salt Lake City, Utah, to San Bernardino, California
                              (exact route from Mississippi through
                              Kentucky to St. Louis is unknown)

←·－·－·← Luzena's route: traveled the California Trail from St. Joseph, Missouri, to
                              Sacramento, California; over the Sierra Nevada
                              via the Carson Route (south of Lake Tahoe) through Placerville

The routes to California taken by three of the bold women featured in this book.

Introduction

No one knows for sure the origin of the name California. Some think it comes from a book known in Europe years before Europeans settled what would become the western United States. Spanish author Garci Rodríguez de Montalvo wrote the romance novel *Las Sergas de Esplandián (The Adventures of Esplandián)*, the first known edition of which appeared in 1510. The book describes a fictional island located "on the right hand of the Indies" named California. The only people who lived there were black women, with Queen Calafia as their leader. The island is described as "one of the strongest in the world, from its steep rocks and great cliffs." The only metal on the island was gold, and griffins and other mythical beasts inhabited this paradise.

So, when a Spanish expedition under the leadership of Hernán Cortés discovered what they thought was an island in 1533 along the west coast of North America, they called it California. In 1539, it was determined that what they had seen was what today we call Baja California, and it is a peninsula, though many maps continued to show California as an island well into the eighteenth century. In 1804, the upper territory became known as Alta California, and the lower was called Baja California province. With the end of the Mexican-American War through the 1848 Treaty of Guadalupe Hidalgo, Alta California became a US territory and part of that territory became the state of California, admitted to the Union on September 9, 1850, as the thirty-first state.

For a state considered to be named after an island inhabited only by women, the stories of remarkable California women were slow to be recognized. Only in the late twentieth century did details about women's accomplishments in California begin to become more widely known and celebrated. Efforts such as museums dedicated specifically to women's history (including one in San Diego, established in 1997), the National Women's History Project (begun in Santa Rosa in 1980), and writers willing to dig through hard-copy records and documents in this digital age all contributed to the recognition of women deserving acclaim. The women in this book made significant contributions to the evolution of California into the powerhouse it is today both nationally and worldwide. Their stories are unique, but each woman made the Golden State a little richer through bold thought and even bolder action.

1
Apolinaria María Guadalupe Lorenzana
(about 1793–1884)

LA BEATA (THE BLESSED ONE)

Excitement was building throughout San Blas, a major shipping port for the Spanish Empire on the Pacific Ocean, in what is now called Mexico. It had been about thirty years since Franciscan friar Father Junípero Serra had ventured into the Province of Las Californias, New Spain, and dedicated the first mission, called San Diego de Alcalá, on July 16, 1769. But people in June 1800 were still fascinated by the conflicting stories they heard about this territory to the north: The native people were hostile—or the natives were being easily converted by the Franciscans and working happily at the established missions. The land was bountiful, with fertile soil everywhere and a perfect climate for crops—or people came close to starvation at times. Since few knew the truth of the situation, a ship leaving for this unknown location generated much interest. On this departure day, many people watched as the ship was loaded with agricultural implements; fabric for a wide variety of clothing, from soldiers' uniforms to religious garb; and adornments for the mission churches. It was whispered that perhaps even a few new priests would go this time.

An hour before the noon departure, the observers noticed a line of people walking down the main street toward the ship. Two adults led the way, followed by twenty children, ten boys and ten girls. The people watching didn't know that twenty-one children had begun the four-hundred-mile walk from Mexico City in November 1799; one had died in the mountains along the way. They were all very young, under the age of ten, and dressed simply and neatly. Unlike most who were so young, they were completely silent, but with eyes large they looked around inquisitively as they approached the ship. The children were *niños expósitos* (abandoned children or orphans) being sent north to be distributed among the settler families in the Spanish pueblos (villages) that had been established in Monterey, Santa Barbara, and San Diego. The boys were supposed to learn useful skills, and the girls were to marry and to remarry if they became widowed. Spain was attempting to increase the Christian population of the northern region, and they hoped these children would eventually raise large families. If this experiment worked, more children would be transported.

After boarding *La Concepción*, a warship with three tall masts and an ironclad hull built at the Ferrol Shipyards in Spain, the children and their two adult companions stood by the railing at the stern of the ship while the final cargo was loaded. The anchor was weighed (raised), and the ship slowly left the harbor. The people on the dock religiously crossed themselves and offered blessings for the *pobrecitos* (poor little ones) who were being sent into such uncertain circumstances.

Each day, under clear skies, the ship sailed closer to Monterey, the first stop. The children quickly became more comfortable in their new surroundings and enjoyed a small degree of unfamiliar freedom but were also quick to react if one of their caretakers noted unseemly behavior. One girl, who appeared to be about seven, one of the youngest of the group, played with the others but still acted very mature. She offered comfort and a kind word to her peers should their games become too rough. She made positive comments about their future and appeared to be the only one of the children truly looking forward to a new life in a new world. Perhaps it was because she had skills many of the other children did not. She could read (though not write), sew simple pieces, make artificial flowers, and figure out basic arithmetic problems. This knowledge probably motivated the eagerness of Apolinaria María Guadalupe Lorenzana to start life in a new place.

———•••———

Born in Mexico City in the early 1790s, Apolinaria had already experienced difficult days. She was left as a baby at the *Real Casa de Expósitos*–the Royal House for Abandoned Children. The institution had been established in 1767 by Archbishop Francisco Lorenzana, so her last name was that of the archbishop, the surname given to all of the foundlings. The name Apolinaria came from a second-century saint. María Guadalupe is the name of the Virgin Mary as used in both the Old World (Europe) and the New World (the Americas). Apolinaria was not considered a pretty girl, but people noted that her face seemed to reflect an inner goodness. The nuns in Mexico City had predicted that she would lead a life devoted to others, and they were extremely sorry to see her leave.

It took several months for the ship to travel the almost 1,670 miles to the pueblo of Monterey. On August 24, the ship cast anchor in the bay by the presidio (fort). Fewer people greeted the ship than had seen its departure, but they were no less eager at its arrival. Embarking passengers were heartily welcomed, and letters were seized and read quickly to learn news about loved ones far away. The cargo started to be unloaded. To the nervous children standing on the deck of the ship, after growing up in Mexico City, Monterey seemed very small–a few houses, a church, the governor's house, and the presidio, all made from adobe (dried mud).

The children watched as a group of people approached. Governor Diego de Borica, the seventh governor of Las Californias from 1794 to 1800, led with six leather-jacketed soldiers from the presidio (formally known as the Royal Presidio of San Carlos de Monterey). He was accompanied by a Franciscan priest who had traveled the six miles from the Mission San Carlos Borromeo del Rio Carmelo to meet the children. The men boarded the ship and greeted the awaiting group. The children humbly responded, and then the party debarked to walk to the mission. It was a long trek, mostly along the shore, and the children were entertained by the ocean waves racing toward them on the beach. They were awed by the cypress trees that the wind had swept into unusual shapes. The plan was that the children would stay at the mission until they were placed in permanent homes, which occurred quickly. Apolinaria later commented that they were given away like puppies. Within two weeks all of the children staying there had been placed, either with families in the Monterey pueblo or in Mission Santa Cruz (across the bay) or in Mission Santa Clara de Asís (inland in the present-day city of Santa Clara, California). Some of the youngest children were sent on to the missions in Santa Barbara and San Diego.

Don José Raimundo Carrillo, a soldier at the Monterey presidio, had arrived in Alta California (the northern part of the Province of Las Californias; Baja was the southern part) as a member of the Gaspar de Portolá expedition in 1769. He had married Tomasa Ygnacia de Lugo, the daughter of another soldier, on April 23, 1781, at Mission San Carlos Borromeo. The wedding ceremony was performed by Father Serra, which was a special honor for the couple due to his importance as the founder of all of the missions. Apolinaria and María de Jesus Torres Lorenzana, the twenty-two-year-old nursemaid of the orphan group, moved into the Carrillo home. The couple had room because their children were grown. Don Carrillo liked Apolinaria. She was not adopted, but she became somewhat of a favored servant who was part of the family. Still, Don Carrillo was not convinced that bringing foundlings to the area was a good idea. He wrote the Viceroy of Mexico: "I do not believe that there are any advantages to be gained by sending more children as these. The inhabitants do not want to take them in, because they have growing families of their own. These children are so unhappy, it seems pointless to take them away from the capital, and expose them to hardship. They are too young."

In Apolinaria's case, this was not true. She was happy during this time in her life. On the trip north, Apolinaria had become attached to María de Jesus and viewed her like a mother. Señora Carrillo was an invalid, so María de Jesus cared for her with Apolinaria's assistance. Though Apolinaria had to work hard, she enjoyed having a home with people who treated her well. She was allowed to attend the school in town, where she read the religious teachings used as texts. She also wanted to know how to write, but writing was not considered a necessary skill for a woman in this time period and was not taught in the school. Apolinaria was determined to learn, however, so she taught herself. She took "empty cigarette papers or a blank piece of paper that somebody had thrown out" and copied pages from whatever books she could find. She carefully drew each letter, memorizing its shape, listening to its sound. When she knew the basics, she tried writing her own thoughts. She later wrote of her efforts: "I managed to learn enough to make myself understood in writing whenever I needed something." Though Apolinaria grew to love the wild natural beauty of the Monterey area, had she been able, she would have left with María de Jesus when her surrogate mother married Miguel Briot, a young artilleryman, in 1802. Apolinaria was devastated when she could not return to Mexico with them. As she related later in life, "That is how I became separated from my mother. I never saw her again. Shortly after she arrived in San Blas my mother died, perhaps from a broken heart because she had to leave me behind."

Father Francisco Pujol (1762–1801) served at Mission San Carlos Borromeo. Like the other missions, its purpose was to support the Spanish troops by planting crops and raising animals to feed the soldiers, in addition to converting the native people to Christianity. He had heard about Apolinaria's devotion to religion, so he watched over her as she grew up. He knew she had rejected offers of marriage, and it did not surprise him when she told him, at age fifteen, that she wanted to become a nun. It was a painful decision for her; she knew the Cabrillo family, especially Señora Cabrillo, would miss her. However, Father Pujol did not feel that being a nun was the right path for Apolinaria. She thought about his advice and decided instead to remain with the Carrillos and begin training to be a nurse at the mission hospital. Apolinaria learned quickly and was soon kept busy by the many patients.

In 1802, Don Carrillo received orders to take over command of the Santa Barbara presidio. Knowing he could be there for many years, he decided to take his family with him. Apolinaria did not welcome this relocation, but she had no choice but to go with the family. Luckily, when they arrived in Santa Barbara, her household duties were terminated and she could spend all of her time acting as a nurse for the hospital at Mission Santa Barbara. She quickly became known for her medical aptitude and received assistance requests from all levels of local citizens as well as from nearby missions—San Buenaventura (Ventura, California), Santa Inés (Solvang, California), and even one in the Los Angeles area (Mission San Gabriel Arcángel). Her expertise as a skilled nurse was eventually recognized throughout the entire mission system, from San Francisco to San Diego. In order to help fill the void of trained women nurses, she started teaching other young women what she had learned about being a competent nurse. But Apolinaria's life was about to change again.

Father Marcos Amestoy, who served at Mission Santa Barbara from 1804 to 1814, asked to see Apolinaria one morning in 1808. He told her that he had heard from Father José Barona at the mission in San Diego that deadly smallpox was spreading throughout the native people of that area and help was badly needed. He asked her to go, and she readily accepted. When Apolinaria arrived, dirty and tired from days of hard riding, she found chaos and immediately took charge. She ordered the families living in the area to feed the sick. She built a central kitchen and had food cooked and taken to the affected people on two-wheeled wooden carts. She instructed servants to take the dead to Mission San Diego de Alcalá, bury them with the appropriate rites, and then burn every piece of their clothing. Under her supervision, the epidemic subsided and lives were saved.

In 1807, Don Carillo had moved to the presidio of San Diego. He served as commandant until 1809, the year he died. He was buried in the chapel on Presidio Hill on November 10, 1809. Apolinaria stayed with his family for a while and then moved in with Sergeant Mariano Mercado and his wife, Dona Josefa Sal, sewing and embroidering to support herself. After Dona Sal's husband died, she opened a school to teach girls how to read and sew, and Apolinaria became a teacher there.

When Apolinaria fell ill and her left hand was temporarily paralyzed, Father José Bernardo Sánchez, who served at Mission San Diego de Alcalá from 1804 to 1820, allowed her to move to that mission to recover. She later recounted, "For the three years that my hand was mangled, I could not work. But in the mission hospital, what I did was cure sick people. Although Father Sánchez had told me that I should not do it myself but should order to have it done, and I should be present to ensure that the servant girls did it well. But as much as I could, I always pitched in and helped the sick." She taught the native women how to sew and launder church vestments and goods. The fathers trusted her to board the ships that brought goods to the town and to make purchases for the missions. She became an assistant housekeeper of the mission.

Mexico won its independence from Spain in 1821. In 1833, the Republic of Mexico ordered all missions to be secularized (taken out of religious control), and church officials thwarted this action by giving away as much of the church's holdings as possible to those who had served faithfully. The padres (priests) at Mission San Diego de Alcalá awarded Apolinaria two ranches—Rancho de Jamacha (Wild Squash Ranch) and La Cañada de Los Coches

The Mission San Diego de Alcalá, where Apolinaria Lorenzana used her medical and organizational skills to help people. –Photographed by Henry F. Withey in December 1936; Library of Congress Prints and Photographs Division, Washington DC

Rancho (Glen of the Hogs Ranch)—for her years of service and devotion to the church. Apolinaria preferred to remain close to the San Diego mission rather than live on her property, which totaled almost nine thousand acres. She built an adobe house at Rancho Jamacha for a caretaker to live in, in addition to a corral and a lime kiln. On the other property, she had a dam built in order to provide water for wheat and barley crops. In 1840, she received an official land grant from Mexican Governor Juan B. Alvarado for Rancho de Jamacha and another one in 1843 from Governor Manuel Micheltorena for La Cañada de Los Coches Rancho. Apolinaria was one of the few women in California to receive a land grant in her name. She later bought a third ranch (Capistrano de Secuán), which was pastureland.

In 1846, Apolinaria traveled to Mission San Luis Rey de Francia (near present-day Oceanside, California) to care for the dying Father José María de Zalvidea. In that same year, the last resident priest at San Diego, Father Vicente Pascual Oliva, moved to Mission San Juan Capistrano, leaving the San Diego mission abandoned. Apolinaria's personal good fortune also began to fade. The United States invaded Mexico in April 1846 and sent troops to occupy southern California. The conflict ended with the Treaty of Guadalupe Hidalgo, signed on February 2, 1848, which called for Mexico to cede to the United States territory that included Apolinaria's land. Although Article 19 of the treaty stated that Mexican Californians "would be maintained and protected in the free enjoyment of their liberty and property," this did not usually happen. The Mexicans did not always understand the many laws and assessments inflicted upon them by the US government due to the language barrier, and many lost their properties. Apolinaria's entire estate was legally seized within the next fifteen years.

In the 1870s, Hubert Howe Bancroft, a noted historian, decided to write about California's early days. He hired five interviewers to talk to 160 elderly people, including Apolinaria, who was now about eighty-four years old. Thomas Savage interviewed her in Santa Barbara in March 1878 and described her: "This old lady residing in Santa Barbara was one of the foundling children sent to California by the Viceroy of Mexico in the early part of this century. . . . She was known by many as Apolinaria la Cuna (the foundling) & by most as la Beata (the pious)."

Apolinaria spoke in Spanish, and Savage wrote down what she said. He asked questions, which then framed her recollections. The final forty-eight-page record has provided much detail about her life as well as events in general of which she was aware. Apolinaria discussed the ins and outs of daily life in the missions, the secularization of the missions, and her negative feelings about California becoming part of the United States. Although she never had children of her own, she spoke with pride that she was godmother to approximately two hundred children from all backgrounds over the course of her life. Some find her recollection confusing, as she talks about coming to California with her mother while church records document that she was an orphan. While Savage attributed this discrepancy to her advanced age, Apolinaria was no doubt referring to María de Jesus Torres Lorenzana. In Apolinaria's mind, María was her mother.

Apolinaria lived out her final years in poverty, supported by the charity of others. As noted in the 1880 census in the Schedules of Defective, Dependent, and Delinquent Classes, she was blind when she died in Santa Barbara in 1884. Her funeral took place at Our Lady of Sorrows Church. The church record, written by Pastor Jaime Vila, reads, "On April 12, 1884, I gave ecclesiastical burial to the body of Apolinaria Lorenzana, single, about one hundred years of age, a native of Mexico whose parents are not known." Our Lady of Sorrows Church still exists today.

Several tributes to Apolinaria can be found in the San Diego area. Avenida Apolinaria is a street in El Cajon, California. In 1949, La Cañada de los Coches Rancho (now in the city of Lakeside) was designated California Historical Landmark No. 425. A plaque was placed at the site of the old gristmill that was built by a later owner. It commemorates this as one of Apolinaria's land grants, at 28.39 acres, the smallest Mexican land grant in California. Today, part of the land is a recreational-vehicle park, which still uses the name Rancho Los Coches. The Women's Museum of California in San Diego maintains a panel of information devoted to Apolinaria's life in its Old Town traveling exhibit.

Apolinaria was featured in a 2013 PBS television documentary series titled *Latino Americans*. Her personal story is intertwined with information about life in the mission system. This video can be viewed online.

While women in the twenty-first century have the opportunity to weigh life options, such as career opportunities and personal relationships, that wasn't generally the case in Apolinaria's era, especially for those without resources and family connections. Today Apolinaria is viewed as a woman who knew what she wanted to do with her life and worked to stay true to those goals. She was the only female foundling in her group to remain unmarried. By refusing to marry and have children, she avoided the confined life that society dictated as acceptable for women at the time. She saw education, both her own and that of others, as a means to a successful life. While she did live within religious doctrines, she enjoyed a degree of freedom and leadership responsibilities in her duties. Only a spirited, courageous woman would have dared to venture outside the normal boundaries for women in those unpredictable early days in California. Apolinaria had that courage and that spirit.

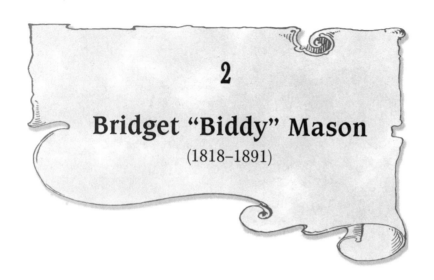

2

Bridget "Biddy" Mason

(1818–1891)

FROM SLAVE TO PHILANTHROPIST

Biddy would have been happy never to see the back end of a cow again! When her master, Robert M. Smith, said he was moving the family west, she didn't realize she would have to walk the entire way. The dust and dirt kicked up by the oxen-drawn wagons stung her eyes and made them water; it was very difficult for Biddy to keep the livestock she had to herd in front of her. In 1847, Robert had become a member of the Church of Jesus Christ of Latter-day Saints, often called the Mormon Church. He and his family joined a group of Mormons living in Fulton, Mississippi, and they all decided to head to the newly established Mormon community in Salt Lake Valley, Utah, that same year. There would be nine white people in the party, including Robert and his wife, Rebecca, and ten slaves, including Biddy and her three daughters: ten-year-old Ellen (born 1838), four-year-old Ann (born 1844), and baby Harriet (born 1847). Biddy's half-sister Hannah also came along. In addition to her livestock responsibilities, thirty-year-old Biddy had to take care of her children (the baby was still nursing and traveled strapped

*Portrait of Biddy
Mason. Unknown date.*
–Schomburg Center for
Research in Black Culture,
Photographs and Prints
Division, New York Public
Library

to Biddy's back), help anyone who became sick or injured during the trip, and deliver any babies born along the way.

The Smith party joined a wagon train being organized by John Brown, a Mormon guide who later became famous for his work as an abolitionist, the name given to people who wanted to abolish slavery. Now there were eleven wagons, fifty-six white people, and thirty-four slaves in the group that became known as the Mississippi Saints. They began the westward trek on March 10, 1848, a cold and rainy day, and they traveled only four miles that day. On the twenty-first of the month, Brown noted this in his journal: "Last night it rained and this morning is very rainy. . . . It is so wet and disagreeable. . . . Some three miles from our camp it assumed the character of a hurricane."

In Kentucky, they traveled west on the National Road and arrived in St. Louis, Missouri, on April 16. There, they bought supplies and joined another group of travelers.

The group followed what would become known as the Mormon Trail. Going through modern-day Iowa, Nebraska, and Wyoming, they discovered that the difficulties of daily life were countered by the delight of seeing new things. They passed great herds of buffalo roaming on the prairie and saw Native Americans for the first time.

It took until October for them to reach the Salt Lake area. Biddy had walked nearly two thousand miles. The family remained in that area for almost three years. Like the other slaves, Biddy worked hard planting and harvesting crops. Although the Mormons accepted black converts, the church had no official law about slavery, either for or against. As church leader Orson Hyde wrote in a Mormon newspaper in 1851, "If there is a sin in selling a slave, let the individual who sells him bear that sin, not the Church." Many Mormons who owned slaves had set them free upon arrival in Utah, but Robert wanted to keep his and resented being criticized for holding people in bondage. So when Brigham Young, the leader of the Mormon Church, asked for volunteers to start a new settlement in California, Robert signed up to go.

Their family wagons were part of the 150 that headed to San Bernardino, in southern California, in 1851. Biddy had to walk again, and this time she walked across the Mojave Desert, where she had to endure sun so hot it felt as if her skin was burning. A lack of water also pushed the group to travel as fast as possible. They probably followed the Mormon Road (which overlapped a portion of the Old Spanish Trail) and if so, they would have stopped to rest at natural springs in a spot that one day would become the city of Las Vegas, Nevada. The San Bernardino Mountains were a huge obstacle, but finally, after another journey of many hundreds of miles, they arrived in San Bernardino in early June. Biddy was tired of walking. She just wanted to stay in California—no matter what.

———•••———

Biddy was born into slavery on August 15, 1818. There is disagreement about where she was born, but her obituary in the *Los Angeles Times* indicated Hancock County, Georgia. Some think her name is short for Bridget, but no one is sure. Biddy was separated from her mother at birth and sold several times, toiling on plantations in Georgia, Mississippi, and South Carolina. Much of her childhood was spent working on John Smithson's plantation in South Carolina. Smithson was a cousin of Rebecca Crosby, who married Robert Smith, and he gave four slaves to Rebecca as a wedding present; among them was Biddy, who was then eighteen years old. The early training Biddy had received using herbs as medicine and practicing as a midwife proved very useful. She often used this knowledge to care for Rebecca Smith, who gave birth to six children in the next twelve years on their plantation in Mississippi near the Gulf of Mexico. Rebecca's health was poor for the rest of her life, so Biddy had to watch over her, especially on the various legs of the journey to California.

California had become a state in 1850. Although it had been admitted to the Union as a free state, where slavery was illegal, there was a legal loophole known as the "in transit" principle. Slave owners could retain their slaves as property if they were in transit through the state, but slave owners quickly realized that local authorities seldom prosecuted landowners who retained their slaves while residing in the state.

The Mormon leadership wanted the settlement at San Bernardino to become an agricultural center where fruit and cotton could be grown and sent back to the Salt Lake Valley community. Smith, however, settled his family along the Santa Ana River, nearer the small town of Los Angeles. He established a ranch with the livestock brought from Utah and added more cattle as he prospered in the next few years. Obviously, Smith was not just passing through!

By 1855, Smith was ready to move again. He'd had a disagreement with the California Mormon leaders, who wanted him to give up some of his land to other church members. Also, antislavery feeling in the state was growing stronger, and he feared that his "in transit" status might soon come under legal review. Then Smith became aware of another California law on the books. Passed in 1852, it stated that people who brought slaves into the state before statehood could keep those slaves if they left the state.

Smith believed this law applied to him because the Smith family and Biddy arrived in California in June 1850 and California became a state on September 9, 1850. Smith was ready to head to Texas, where slavery was legal.

In December 1855, Smith took his entire household up into the Santa Monica Mountains. The women and children slept in wagons, and the men rested on the cold ground. Why did they leave a comfortable ranch if they were not ready to start for Texas? It seems as if Smith wanted to isolate his slaves so that they could not escape before his planned date of departure, January 1, 1856.

In the meantime, Elizabeth Flake Rowan, a free black woman who was a friend of Biddy's, advised the Los Angeles County sheriff that Smith was taking slaves to Texas. Sheriff Frank DeWitt obtained a writ of habeas corpus (which required the parties involved in the dispute to come before a judge) to prevent Smith from taking all of his slaves out of state until a court hearing on the matter could occur. He and the sheriff of San Bernardino County found the Smith party, and Biddy, her children, and the other slaves were taken to the Los Angeles jail. They were not under arrest but were being held in safekeeping until their situation could be examined legally.

The case went before Judge Benjamin Hayes of the Los Angeles District Court. Smith may have been hopeful of a favorable outcome since Hayes was from Maryland, a state where slavery was allowed. Smith's attorney argued that Biddy and the other black people in Smith's party were members of his family—not slaves—and that they had come willingly with the Smiths from Mississippi. Smith claimed that he had "supported them ever since, subjecting them to no greater control than his own children, and not holding them as slaves." Since California law prohibited a black person from testifying in court against a white individual, Judge Hayes talked with Biddy in his chambers.

After a three-day hearing, the judge decided that he had satisfactory proof that Biddy and the other slaves were indeed being held against their will and decreed that "all of the said persons of color are entitled to their freedom, and are free and cannot be held in slavery or involuntary servitude." He based his decision on the following:

> And it further appearing to the satisfaction of the judge here that the said Robert Smith intended to and is about to remove from the State of California where slavery does not exist, to the State of Texas, where slavery of Negroes and persons of color does exist, and is established by the municipal laws, and intends to remove the said before-mentioned persons of color, to his own use without the free will and consent of all or any of the said persons of color, whereby their liberty will be greatly jeopardized, and there is good reason to apprehend and believe that they may be sold into slavery or involuntary servitude.

Therefore, on January 19, 1856, Biddy, at age thirty-seven, became a free woman, along with her children and all of Robert Smith's other slaves. The timing was fortunate; in 1857, the US Supreme Court, in the Dred Scott decision, invalidated the laws that freed slaves when they moved to free states or territories.

Smith and his wife, Rebecca, and their children moved to Texas, where he was later excommunicated in absentia from the Mormon Church for his "un-Christian" conduct.

Biddy and her daughters were invited to stay with the family of Robert Owens, a free black man who was a successful businessman in Los Angeles and had assisted Elizabeth Rowan in gaining Biddy's freedom. Ten months later, on October 16, 1856, Biddy's eldest daughter, Ellen, married Robert's son Charles.

But now in January, right after she was freed, Biddy had to make a living. She worked for a while as a household domestic. Then, since she had medical skills, Dr. John Strother Griffin, the brother-in-law of Judge Hayes, made her his assistant in 1859. She is reported to have been paid $2.50 per day, an excellent wage for the time period. Dr. Griffin served as the doctor for the county hospital, but for expectant mothers who did not want to go to the hospital to deliver their babies, Biddy ran a midwife service. This earned her even more money, or if the mother's family did not have cash, Biddy was paid in vegetables, chickens, eggs, or other food. Though she bravely cared for people during a smallpox epidemic in 1857, helping many people, she was unable to save her daughter Ann, who died of the disease in August of that year.

Biddy started to use the last name "Mason" around 1860. She may have felt she needed a last name so patients would view her more professionally, but no one knows why she selected this name. It may have been the name of the family who owned the property on which she was born. Or she may have chosen it because it was the middle name of Amasa Mason Lyman, one of the Mormon guides on the trip to California. He later became mayor of San Bernardino, and Biddy had visited his household. Whatever the reason for her choice, Biddy was now usually called Grandma Mason. She was well known and well liked by the people of Los Angeles—especially the poor. Biddy could be seen on the streets at all hours with her big black bag of midwife supplies, which also always contained a certified copy of Judge Hayes's ruling making her free. Biddy wasn't taking any chances.

Biddy was also careful with her money. After ten years, she had saved $250, and on November 28, 1866, she bought property at the edge of town on Spring Street. She was the first black woman to own land in Los Angeles.

She gardened on the property, which she referred to as "the Homestead," and then built a house at 331 Spring Street, which she rented out for additional income as she still lived with the Owens family. In 1884, she sold part of her land for $1,500 and used the money to build a two-story building on the other section. She lived on the second floor and rented out the storerooms on the lower level. Her house became a haven for homeless people and others who needed help. In 1885, her two grandsons, Robert Curry Owens and Henry L. Owens, started a livery stable on another part of her property, which Biddy had deeded to them for $10 and "love and affection." Biddy kept working and saving and buying property. By investing shrewdly, she became the wealthiest African American woman in Los Angeles by the late 1800s. Although she never learned to read or write, she became fluent in Spanish and sometimes dined at the home of Pío Pico, a wealthy Los Angeles landowner who had been the last governor of California under Mexican rule.

Biddy watched Los Angeles grow over the years and wanted to contribute in some way. In 1872, she held a meeting at her house to establish, with her daughter Ellen and son-in-law Charles Owens, the Los Angeles First African Methodist Episcopal (AME) Church. The church began in her home but soon moved to its own building, on land that Biddy donated. When church funds were low, she paid the minister's salary and the taxes on the building out of her own pocket. The church still exists, although now at a different location (2270 South Harvard Boulevard). The Los Angeles Board of Education was allowed to share the original site, and it opened the first school for black children in the church building. In the 1880s, after a flood wiped out many homes in the area, Biddy paid for the groceries for those displaced whether they were white or black. People lined up at her door, seeking assistance from the woman who believed that "if you hold your hand closed, nothing good can come in. The open hand is blessed, for it gives in abundance, even as it receives."

Only when she became extremely frail in her later years did she have her grandson stand at the door and turn people away.

Biddy died on January 15, 1891, at age seventy-two. Only a simple funeral was held before she was buried in an unmarked grave at Evergreen Cemetery in the Boyle Heights section of Los Angeles. In 1988, the First AME Church of Los Angeles that she helped create wanted to recognize Biddy as a philanthropist and humanitarian for all she had done for the community. They erected a monument on her grave that gave the dates of her birth and death and then listed all the ways she would be remembered:

Former slave
Philanthropist
Humanitarian
Founding Member
First African Methodist
Episcopal Church
1872
Los Angeles, California

About three thousand people showed up for the monument's dedication on Palm Sunday, March 27, 1988. One of those present was Los Angeles Mayor Tom Bradley, the first African American mayor of the city. He remarked, "She is an example of the courage of black women in the early days of this city. Our young people need to know about her." In that same year, Biddy was highlighted in an exhibit titled "Black Angelenos" at the California African American Museum in Los Angeles.

Biddy's Los Angeles neighborhood looks a lot different today than it did in 1851, when she first saw it. Now it is a bustling commercial center in the heart of the city. But Biddy's presence is still there. The National Endowment for the Humanities supported two public art projects on the site of her Spring Street home, which is now known as the Biddy Mason Monument Urban Park. On November 16, 1989, designated Biddy Mason Day in Los Angeles (and now celebrated annually), the first art piece was unveiled. Designed by Sheila Levrant de Bretteville and entitled *Biddy Mason: Time and Place*, it is an eighty-foot poured concrete wall outside the Broadway Spring Center (a ten-story retail and garage complex), upon which words and images (midwife's bag, scissors, spools of thread) relating to Biddy Mason's life are affixed. One of the people attending the ceremony was Biddy's great-great-great-granddaughter Linda Cox. As later reported in the *Los Angeles Times* (on July 31, 1991, when she helped open the actual park at the

Broadway Spring Center), she commented, "It took one hundred years for Biddy Mason to be recognized, but we walk a lot taller knowing this history."

The other artwork, which was unveiled in 1990, is displayed inside the Broadway Spring Center and is seen as the elevator doors open from the parking structure. Called *House of the Open Hand* and designed by Betye Saar, it includes a photo panel of the actual front porch of Biddy's home with wooden siding, a picket fence, and a window. Saar described her intent: "I wanted to capture an intimate feeling within this space. I hoped to give an emotional link through the window, which I call a Memory Window."

Biddy Mason was inducted into the California Social Work Hall of Distinction in 2002, and her story is now being incorporated into school textbooks about California history. Visitors to the Autry Museum of the American West in Los Angeles, between April 25, 2015, and January 3, 2016, saw her recognized in its display "Empire and Liberty: The Civil War and the West." The First AME Church of Los Angeles continues her work through the Biddy Mason Charitable Foundation. Hopefully, Biddy's story will continue to be presented as a testament to what one person can achieve when given the opportunity. For that is the true legacy of this remarkable woman.

3

Luzena Stanley Hunt Wilson

(1819–1902)

GOLD RUSH ENTREPRENEUR

Luzena Stanley Hunt Wilson sighed heavily. Her body felt exhausted, but her mind was greatly relieved. After long months of grueling cross-country travel in a bumpy wagon, she, her husband, Mason, and two small sons, Jay and Thomas, along with the family cow, had finally arrived in Sacramento, California. Luzena noted, "My poor tired babies were asleep on the mattress in the bottom of the wagon, and I peered out into the gathering gloom, trying to catch a glimpse of our destination." The date was September 30, 1849.

Although it was evening, the place was teeming with activity. Several thousand people, mostly men, went about their business. The muddy streets were congested with horses and mules coming in or going out to nearby gold diggings. There were only a few wooden buildings, and numerous tents were being used for shelter. Campfires illuminated the dark just enough to see some residents rolled up in blankets for the night. Others played cards. Merchants sold their wares from a board placed across two barrels. Each board held a scale to determine payment. Coins were rare, so gold dust

Luzena and daughter Correnah in the 1880s. –Used with permission of Rosemarie Mossinger

was used to pay for goods and services. Everything cost at least $1 because that's how much a pinch of dust was worth. The quality of items, especially food, was questionable because most things were brought in by ship around Cape Horn in South America from the US East Coast (which could take as long as a year). Foods such as salt pork and flour were often spoiled by the time they reached California.

Luzena was somewhat embarrassed as they rode through the town. Men openly stared at her; it had been months since many of them had seen a woman. Luzena didn't think she looked very good after the long journey: "My skirts were torn off in rags above the ankles; my sleeves hung in tatters above my elbows; my hands, brown and hard, were gloveless; around my neck was tied a cotton square, torn from a discarded dress; the soles of my leather shoes had long ago parted with the uppers."

But an incident the night before in the foothills proved that her appearance didn't matter. She had been approached by a hungry miner as she was cooking a biscuit for her family over a campfire. He offered her $5 for the biscuit, and when she hesitated, he doubled his offer (equivalent to more than $300 in 2016). The miner said he really wanted bread made by a woman. She accepted the gold piece. That night, she dreamed about miners who struck gold, and each one gave a share to her. Luzena had gold fever! But she realized it was her cooking, not mining, that would make her rich in California.

———•••———

Luzena Stanley Hunt was born May 1, 1819, to Asa and Diana Hunt, Quakers who worked a lumber mill making planks and boards in North Carolina (near present-day Greensboro). She was their third child, but only one sister, Lydia, was still alive when she was born. Six more children followed, four girls and two boys, so Luzena was kept busy helping to care for them. Though the Quakers expected strict adherence to their customs, the Hunts did not always obey. Asa was disowned from the Quakers in 1830 for distilling spirits and taking an oath to serve in a civil jury. Diana and daughters Lydia and Luzena were disowned in February 1836 for not attending meeting and for wearing clothes considered too fancy for the group's standards. The family is not mentioned again in the records of the New Garden Meeting, so they must not have ever sought readmission to the Quakers.

In 1843, the Hunts moved to Andrew County, Missouri, located in the northwest part of the state. Working under the Preemption Act of 1841, they acquired 160 acres from the federal government. This allowed settlers who lived on their property for fourteen months to purchase it from the government for as little as $1.25 an acre before it was offered for public sale. To preserve ownership, the person had to improve the land in some way, either by building some type of structure or clearing the land for farming.

Luzena married Mason Wilson on December 19, 1844. Aside from his birthplace (Union County, Kentucky) and his birth date (October 3, 1806), little is known about his early life.

After their marriage the couple bought land and settled in a log cabin on the grassy prairie near Luzena's parents. Their first son, Thomas Stanley, was born on September 21, 1845, and their second, Jay Crittenden, on June 20, 1848. When news of the gold strike in California reached them, nothing could keep Mason in Missouri. He meant to go to California alone, but Luzena would not hear of it. "I would not be left behind. I thought where he could go I could go, and where I went I could take my two little toddling babies. . . . I little realized then the task I had undertaken."

The Wilsons left on May 1, 1849, abandoning their land and cabin in Missouri. Probably relying on Joseph Ware's *The Emigrants' Guide to California* as direction of what to expect, they packed their wagon and readied their cow for the trip. That first day of travel, they made it across the Missouri River and into Indian Territory. Luzena had to quell her fears:

> I had read and heard whole volumes of their [the Indians'] bloody deeds, the massacre of harmless white men, torturing helpless women, carrying away captive innocent babes. I felt my children the most precious in the wide world, and I lived in an agony of dread the first night. The Indians were friendly, of course . . . but I, in the most tragic-comic manner, sheltered my babies with my own body, and felt imaginary arrows pierce my flesh a hundred times during the night.

Like many others, she found that "some things . . . [considered] necessities when we started became burdensome luxuries, and before many days . . . dropped by the road-side." The routine of the trip became extremely tiresome. Only a broken-down wagon or difficult river crossing offered any relief. It took them three months to reach what Luzena called "the most formidable of all the difficulties": forty miles of searing hot desert that stretched southwest from the Humboldt Sink to the Carson River (present-day Nevada). "It was a forced march over the alkali plain, lasting three days, and we carried with us the water that had to last, for both men and animals, till we reached the other side. The hot earth scorched our feet; the grayish dust hung about us like a cloud, making our eyes red, and tongues parched, and our thousand bruises and scratches smart like burns."

Following what was known as the Carson Route, the Wilsons went through Hangtown (now Placerville, California) before reaching Sacramento.

The Wilsons found that life moved quickly in Sacramento. Businesses opened and closed due to the lure of getting rich quickly in the Gold Rush. Within three days of their arrival, the Wilsons sold their oxen for $600 at the Horse Market and bought a share in the Trumbow (spelled Trumbo in a city directory) House hotel, one of the few wooden buildings in the town. Luzena described it as "a story-and-a-half building which stood . . . close to what was then the Commercial Exchange, Board of Trade and Chamber of Commerce." The hotel had a long living room that served as a dormitory. Rows and rows of bunk beds were stacked against the walls from floor to ceiling. The kitchen became Luzena's special place. While some foodstuffs were locally produced, much came in by ship. Sweet potatoes, oranges, and lemons arrived from the Sandwich Islands (now Hawaii) and flour came from the East Coast or Chile. After such a journey, it was no wonder that food packaged in tins (such as sardines) or jars (fruit and pickles) arrived in the best condition.

Overall, life was going well for the Wilson family. After two months, the couple sold their hotel interest for $1,000 and moved into a canvas house a little way down the street. They put all their cash into barley, which they purchased for 15¢ per pound, and kept the bags in a pile on the ground next to their house. Barley was a favored food for mules, so the Wilsons knew it would sell to the gold miners, or '49ers, as they were known.

Unfortunately, it rained a lot that year. One day in December, a cry went out that a levee had broken. Mason ran to help at the breach, as Sacramento was located below the water level of nearby rivers. Warm weather started to thaw the snow in the mountains early, and on January 9, 1850, that caused a real problem. Luzena was cooking supper over a campfire when she first noticed small streams of water swirling about her feet. Quickly the water rose to inches. Luzena raced the children to the safety of the hotel and then hurried back to try to rescue their things. Soon she was fighting water knee deep. In an hour, the whole town was afloat. Forty people, including the Wilson family, remained on the second story

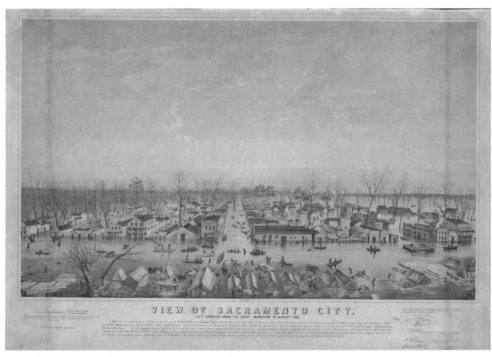

Sacramento City as it appeared during the great inundation in January 1850. –Drawn by Geo. W. Casilear and Henry Bainbridge; Library of Congress Prints and Photographs Division, Washington DC

of the hotel for seventeen days, trapped by water that fluctuated between ten and twenty feet deep, depending on the flow from the hills. They ate raw onions and anything else they could catch as it floated by. Driftwood was burned for heat and cooking.

When the Wilsons were finally able to get back to their house, they realized they were ruined. The bags of barley had burst and sprouted. Luzena was terrified of another flood and wanted to relocate to higher ground. When she heard about a gold strike in an area called Deer Creek Dry Diggings in the Sierra Nevada foothills, she convinced Mason to move there. The settlement around these mines began to be called Nevada in March 1850 and Nevada City beginning in 1861.

But how would they get to Nevada City? It was sixty miles away, and there were no real roads between it and Sacramento. They had no money to pay for transport, but Luzena found an idle teamster and made a bargain. He would transport her, the children, her stove, and two sacks of flour to Nevada City for $700 but would not demand payment immediately. Luzena promised she would pay him if she stayed alive and made money. Mason would walk and drive the cow (who had somehow survived the flood) to their new home.

The winter rain and snow had turned the path they followed into mud, and the wagon kept getting stuck. It was a miserable twelve-day journey. Luzena was thankful when she finally saw the canvas tents at the new mining camp in March.

Upon arrival, Luzena first made sure everyone vigorously scrubbed off the grime of the trip. Then the family needed shelter. They collected tree limbs and other brush and undergrowth, which they wove together to construct a primitive house. The stove was placed nearby under a large pine tree. Luzena soon decided to take in boarders as a means of income:

> I bought two boards from a precious pile belonging to a man who was building the second wooden house in town. With my own hands I chopped stakes, drove them into the ground, and set up

31

my table. I bought provisions at a neighboring store, and when my husband came back at night he found, [a]mid the weird light of the pine torches, twenty miners eating at my table. Each man as he rose put a dollar in my hand and said I might count him as a permanent customer. I called my hotel "El Dorado."

In six weeks, Luzena made enough money to pay her debt to the teamster. The Wilsons earned enough to build a wooden house and kept adding rooms as their business of taking in boarders grew. Luzena took her husband in as a business partner as she bragged, "We had then from seventy-five to two hundred boarders at twenty-five dollars a week. I became luxurious and hired a cook and waiters. Maintaining only my position as managing housekeeper, I retired from active business in the kitchen."

This gave Luzena time to do "little pieces of sewing for the men." She and Mason opened a store and within six months, they had $10,000 invested in the hotel and store. They also owned a stock of goods worth about the same amount. Luzena's kitchen acted as a bank vault for their money and that of their boarders. She noted at one time there were two milk pans piled high with bags of gold dust. She also slept with gold dust under her mattress. Luzena decided to try lending out money to earn more, but this was not as profitable. "I loaned the money, but at such an extravagant rate of interest that I might have foreseen that my man must fail and run away, which he finally did. I believe the rate of interest at which I loaned it was ten percent a month."

Luzena thrived in this masculine environment because there were so few women. As she noted, "Even I have had men come forty miles over the mountains just to look at me, and I never was called a handsome woman in my best days, even by my most ardent admirers."

Nevada City provided a comfortable home for the Wilson family. There were two churches, two theaters, a post office, hotels, boarding houses, and restaurants. There was even a bullring where bear and bull fights occurred on Sunday afternoons. Once again, however, the Wilsons' security did not last. This time it was not by water but by fire. On March 12, 1851, flames were observed at about one in the morning in a pile of burned pine shavings, which people thought had been extinguished. By daybreak, the fire had destroyed 150 structures, according to the report in the *Sacramento Transcript* newspaper. All that remained of the town was ashes. Luzena and her family had "stood with bated breath and watched the fiery monster crush in his great red jaws the homes we toiled to build. The tinder-like pine houses ignited with a spark, and the fire raged and roared over the fated town. . . . The eight thousand inhabitants were homeless . . . and most of them were penniless as well."

Lucky for the Wilsons, Mason had $500 in his pockets, but even this small comfort was not enough to keep Luzena well. Exhaustion and worry took their toll. Racked with fever, she rested for weeks in the home of a miner who had a cabin in the woods. When she regained her health, the family decided to return to Sacramento, selling their property to a miner. To add to their despair, he found thousands of dollars worth of gold on the site.

Reaching Sacramento, the Wilsons were surprised by all that had changed. Another flood had occurred while they were in Nevada City, so brick buildings had replaced the tents, and wooden sidewalks helped people avoid the mud and dust. Well-stocked stores offered a variety of goods. The Pony Express delivered mail every day, and stagecoaches left to carry people and freight all over the area. There was even the first permanent theater to be built in the state of California, the Eagle Theatre. Although the January 1850 flood had destroyed it, the theater was soon reconstructed and is still located on Front Street in the historic Old Sacramento area.

But Luzena and Mason decided not to stay in Sacramento. They wanted to try their luck in California's farming region. They crossed the Sacramento River at Knights Landing (which still exists as a town in Yolo County) and headed south into the Vaca Valley. The Vaca and the Peña families had been among the earliest white settlers in this area. They had been given Rancho Los Putos as a land grant (44,385 acres) from Mexico in 1843. While many holders of Mexican land grants planted grain and food crops, the Vaca-Peña land was dedicated to cattle ranching. The Wilsons stopped there. Mason went to work cutting oat hay (it was selling in San Francisco for $150 a ton) while Luzena set up her camp stove again, this time under an oak tree. Using a burnt stick to write, she put up a sign that read "Wilson's Hotel." Luzena described this new pursuit: "The boards from the wagon bed made my table, handy stumps and logs made comfortable chairs, and the guest tethered his horse at the distance of a few yards and retired to the other side of the hay-stack to sleep. The next morning he paid me a dollar for his bed and another one for breakfast . . . and rode away, feeling he had not paid too dearly for his entertainment."

Again, Luzena was successful and her hotel was soon known as the best on the route between Benicia (the capital of California from February 11, 1853, to February 25, 1854) and Sacramento. It was close to the Vaca adobe house, which was destroyed by an earthquake in 1892; the Peña Adobe still stands and is California Historical Landmark No. 534. Living among mostly vaqueros (Spanish-speaking cowboys), Luzena thought nothing of traveling miles on horseback to visit another female who spoke English. But she and Mason were often invited to attend dances and feasts given by their Spanish neighbors. She appreciated the brilliant colors the women wore and enjoyed the stews spiced with hot chiles, tortillas, and "tolerable whisky." Luzena once described Juan Manuel Vaca as the "lord of the soil." Over his holdings roamed cattle and mustangs, and "a whole day's hard riding about the grant would not reveal half the extent of [his] four-footed possessions."

The Wilsons' plan had been to buy land and settle on it. They originally bought two hundred acres near Alamo Creek, and later various properties in the town that became known as Vacaville. But a dispute arose about their property lines because it had been part of the original Vaca-Peña land grant, and they had to fight off squatters who tried to take their holdings. A State Lands Commission was formed to try to sort out land disputes. It took until June 1858, when President James Buchanan signed a patent for the Vaca land grant, that Mason and Luzena's land issues were settled. Their hotel eventually evolved into a two-story brick building located at the corner of Main and Davis Streets in Vacaville. Construction was completed in October 1858. In addition to helping Luzena with the hotel, Mason became an agent for Wells Fargo & Company, and over time, the Wilsons became one of the wealthiest families in Solano County.

Luzena had two more children while all of this was occurring. Mason Junior was born January 12, 1855, and daughter Correnah Morehead arrived on April 24, 1857. The need to educate her children forced Luzena to help establish a local school. She also took over the medical needs of the community. Using a medicine chest left by a doctor who failed to prosper in the area and who paid his hotel bill with his wares, Luzena dosed people with calomel and quinine. She remarked, "I grew so familiar with the business that I almost fancied myself a genuine doctor. I don't think I ever killed anybody, and I am quite sure I cured a good many of my patients."

Although the Wilsons had finally found financial success, Mason became restless. Early in 1867, he took a trip to Texas and upon his return he tried, without success, to sell his California holdings. In December 1872, he abandoned his family and returned to Texas. The local newspaper reported that Luzena received a letter "informing her that she would probably never see him again; that all he had was hers during her lifetime, but that he wished it to go to their two youngest children at her death." Luzena never did see Mason again, and their son Jay went to Texas to live with his father.

Luzena dedicated the rest of her days to business. She had about six hundred acres at this time and decided to turn them into orchards. She managed the hotel until 1874, when she sold it for $6,000. Luzena also tried her hand at lending out money again, this time with more success.

In June 1877, Luzena and Correnah took a trip to Yosemite. They arrived home to find disaster had struck yet again. A fire had started in their barn and spread quickly, burning down half of the town. Luzena lost all of her possessions, including the first Steinway piano in Solano County. When subsequent fires also ruined her wheat fields and several houses she owned, Luzena decided, as she had in the past, to move. Since Mason Junior was working in San Francisco, Luzena, Correnah, and Thomas joined him there. She and Correnah lived in various residences before Correnah's marriage in 1886. In 1888, Luzena and Thomas moved into the Hotel Pleasanton. For the rest of her life, Luzena lived in someone else's hotel.

Correnah had become very ill in 1881. To help pass the time while Correnah was recuperating, Luzena told stories of her early days in California, perhaps for this reason:

> The rags and tatters of my first days in California are well nigh forgotten in the ease and plenty of the present. . . . The years have been full of hardships, but they have brought me many friends, and my memory of them is rich. . . . The dear old friends are falling asleep one by one, many of them already lying at rest under the friendly flower-strewn California sod; day by day the circle narrows, and in a few more years there will be none of us left to talk over the "early days."

Correnah was enthralled and wrote down in longhand her mother's recollections. They were published as a series of articles in a San Francisco newspaper, the *Argonaut*, between February and April of 1881, but no one knew it was Luzena's story. The articles, titled "A Woman's Reminiscences of Early Days," were identified only as having been written by "W." Years later, Correnah typed and bound her mother's stories into a book. She presented it to the library at Mills College, her alma mater. This is why today we have so many examples of Luzena's actual thoughts about her life in California.

Luzena became a widow when Mason died September 5, 1882. He is buried in Naler Cemetery in Moody, Texas. She turned over her business holdings to Thomas in 1883 and traveled. She and Correnah began a yearlong trip to Europe later that year. This time Luzena traveled across the country in the luxury of a railroad car instead of bumping around in a covered wagon. She always had fond memories of her years in the Vacaville area and often visited the Vaca Valley. Her last visit in November 1901 was noted in the *Vacaville Reporter*: "Mrs. Wilson has not visited Vacaville for several years and expresses surprise at the splendid growth it has made since her last visit. She was one of the earliest settlers, coming here in 1851."

Luzena died July 11, 1902, in San Francisco, reportedly of thyroid cancer. Her ashes are held in the Corona Room at the San Francisco Columbarium. When the Panama-Pacific International Exposition was held in San Francisco in 1915, celebrating the completion of the Panama Canal, Correnah served as a director on the women's board that helped establish the California Host Building. She also honored her mother and other pioneer women by supporting the creation of the Pioneer Mother Monument. This $25,000 bronze sculpture, created by sculptor Charles Grafly, had a prominent place during the exposition in the Palace of Fine Arts, a building that still stands today thanks to careful restoration. The plaque at the base of the sculpture reads:

> Over rude paths, beset with hunger and risk, she pressed on toward the vision of a better country. To an assemblage of men busied with the perishable rewards of today, she brought the threefold leaven of enduring society faith, gentleness, hope, with the nurture of children.

The statue was placed outside in Golden Gate Park in 1940 near the Pioneer Log Cabin, which has stood in the park since 1911.

Luzena was honored in a display at the Oakland Museum of California as part of the sesquicentennial celebration of the Gold Rush and of California becoming a state in 1850. She also was featured in the 2006 PBS American Experience documentary titled *The Gold Rush*.

The Wilsons are commemorated in Vacaville with designated streets. Wilson and Mason Streets cross near Ulatis Creek (Luzena used water from the creek to keep fresh the milk from the cow that came west with them) and Andrews Park. The latter sits on land traded by Mason with the Methodist Episcopal Church as the site for Pacific Methodist College. Jay, Mason Junior, and Correnah all attended the Preparatory Department's classes at that school. Luzena also has an avenue named for her nearby.

While there are many accounts of the Gold Rush (and subsequent eras in California) written from men's perspectives, there are fewer recollections from women. From Luzena, we get a true picture of what it was like. "Yes, we worked; we did things that our high-toned servants would now look at aghast, and say it was impossible for a woman to do. But the one who did not work in '49 went to the wall. It was a hand-to-hand fight with starvation at first."

No matter the obstacles over the years, Luzena never gave up. Perhaps it was her Quaker upbringing or just personal tenacity, but she met each setback in her life with resolve. She would just start over again. In the end (and without her husband), she rose to a prominent place in California society. She was listed in the 1888 *San Francisco Blue Book*, which contained "the names, addresses, reception days, and country residences of the elite of San Francisco, San Rafael, Sausalito, San Mateo, Redwood City, Menlo Park, San Jose." For example, it noted that Mrs. L. S. Wilson was available for callers on Mondays. In 1900, she had her portrait done by Oscar Kunath, who painted many of the well-to-do in the city, including Mrs. Leland Stanford whose husband served as governor of California (1862–1863) and in the US Senate (1885–1893). While most rags-to-riches stories from this era have a masculine main character, Luzena shows us that it was a possible transformation for a woman as well.

4
Nellie Elizabeth Pooler Chapman
(1847–1906)

THE LADY FIXED THEIR TEETH

It was obvious that the man was in pain. He held a handkerchief to his cheek, but this was nothing new to dentist Dr. Allen Chapman. He escorted the patient into the front parlor of the house at 227 Sacramento Street in Nevada City, California. The man placed his cowboy hat on the hook on the wall and noticed the petite, smartly dressed woman watching him from the corner of the room. Dr. Chapman introduced the woman as his wife, Nellie. The man acknowledged her, but it was apparent that the discomfort of a bad tooth held his attention.

Because people in the West in the late 1800s were very self-reliant, Dr. Chapman knew that his patient must have already tried some of the remedies commonly used to treat a toothache. These included drinking lime water in which Peruvian bark from the cinchona tree was soaked overnight. We now know that this bark contains quinine, which had been used for centuries for relief of toothache. Drinking tea made from watercress and rubbing whiskey onto the gums near the affected tooth were also typical practices. A poultice made of mashed ginger or a rag soaked in clove oil also could be placed on a tooth to reduce pain. The man might have purchased Cocaine Toothache Drops. Made by the Lloyd Manufacturing Company, these were readily available and even given to children and babies as a pain reliever (cocaine was not banned in the United States until 1914). Dr. Chapman hoped

Portrait of Nellie Pooler Chapman.
–Used with permission of Searls Historical Library, Nevada City

his patient was smart enough to know that scratching his gums with an iron nail until they bled and then driving the nail into a wooden board would not stop pain, as many folks believed. But whatever he might have tried had not worked because here he was in the dentist's office.

Nellie wondered if the man had seen the label "Imperial Columbia" in gold script on the back of the red velvet chair because he brushed the dust off his clothes before he sat down. His eyes darted around the room. A round stool covered with red-and-white cut velvet in a floral pattern stood next to his chair. On a stand rested a porcelain bowl and a holder for a crystal water glass. In the corner of the room, a tray of instruments, including one that looked like a corkscrew, lay on a large wooden cabinet. The titles of the books in view through the windows in the cabinet doors included an 1875 copy of *The Principles and Practice of Dental Surgery* (a 794-page book written by Chapin Aaron Harris) and the 1878 edition of *Gray's Anatomy, Descriptive and Surgical.*

Nellie knew this man anticipated that her husband would care for him. But Allen excused himself, saying that he had to leave to get to Virginia City, Nevada. The man looked stunned. Nellie wondered how she should calm his fears. Should she tell him about the state-of-the-art dental equipment that surrounded him? The tall metal object with a treadle base and flywheel with a metal rod at the end of a wire was a dental engine, the most modern dental drill on the market at that time. When a foot pushed on the treadle, the flywheel rotated and provided the energy to power the drill. There was also an aspirator, used to pull saliva from the mouth. The corkscrew tool allowed the user to place it securely around a tooth and pull it out efficiently; extraction was the most common dental practice. The petite woman smoothed her apron and decided it was time to break the news to the man that she was the one who would be taking care of his toothache.

———•••———

Born on May 9, 1847, in Norridgewock, Maine, Nellie Elizabeth Pooler had never dreamed about a career as a dentist. Her father, John Ruxton Pooler, was born in Ireland and became a US citizen in 1840. The Gold Rush in California captured her father's curiosity, so off he went, arriving in California in 1852. Two years later, Nellie traveled with her Canadian-born mother, Mathilda J. O'Hara Pooler, through the Isthmus of Panama to reach Nevada, California. ("City" was added to the town's name in 1861 to prevent confusion with the Nevada Territory that was created on March 2 of that year. Nevada City will be used here for clarity). Her father was working in the Gold Flat Mine. He stayed with mining for eight years before he tried farming.

Dr. Allen Chapman was born November 14, 1826, in Hebron (Washington County), New York. His parents, William and Rebecca Allen Chapman, came from families that had been in what became the United States long before the American Revolution. Allen arrived in Nevada City two years after Nellie, having sailed on the ship *George Law* from New York to the Isthmus of Panama. From there, he crossed to the Pacific side and traveled to San Francisco on another ship, finally arriving in Nevada City in April 1856, bringing $10,000 worth of dental equipment with him. Having begun studying dentistry at the age of seventeen with Dr. Nelson D. Ross, Allen had practiced the profession in Ross's office in Troy, New York, for the prior thirteen years (1843–1856). Worn down by the strain, he decided to head to California, where he figured there would be less stress, and it would also allow him to search for gold. The town of Nevada City had just incorporated (April 19, 1856), so he decided that a mining town would be an ideal location to open a dental office. Unfortunately, the worst fire Nevada City had ever experienced occurred on July 19, 1856, just three months after Allen arrived. It burned four hundred buildings, including four churches, the new courthouse, and all of the county records. Ten people lost their lives. Dr. Chapman's dental equipment was totally destroyed, so he had to replace it. He thought it would be a sound investment because in 1856 Nevada City was actually the third-largest city in California (after San Francisco and Sacramento), with around ten thousand residents.

Allen was fortunate that he had the resources to start again. Many practicing dentistry in this time period could not afford residential offices and had to move from town to town seeking patients. Most had little training other than apprenticeships; the first dental school in the nation, the Baltimore College of Dental Surgery in Maryland, hadn't opened until 1840. Allen established a dental office on the second floor of the Kidd-Knox Building, which was rebuilt in brick after the fire and still stands today on the corner of Broad and Pine Streets in Nevada City. An announcement of the opening of his practice was published in the local newspaper on October 22, 1856. And on January 4, 1861, the *Nevada Journal* announced that Dr. James H. Hatch, who had come to California from Vermont, had become Allen's business partner. The 1880 US census listed Dr. Hatch in San Francisco, so their partnership must have terminated at some point.

There is no record of how Nellie and Allen met, but it was probably through her father. When she was fourteen, she married the thirty-four-year-old, bearded dentist at the Red Castle, a four-story Gothic Revival–style mansion located at the top of Prospect Hill overlooking the town. Built in 1860, it derived its name from its brick construction and white wooden trim that gave the appearance of icicles. The family home then of John and Abigail Williams, it was later used as a bed-and-breakfast inn for many years before it closed in 2014. After the wedding on March 24, 1861, Dr. Chapman and his bride soon became neighbors of the Williams family. Between 1862 and 1864, they built the house at 227 Sacramento Street on the southwest side of the street facing Deer Creek. Allen used his home address in his advertising (such as in this 1867 example):

Dr. A. Chapman
Surgical and Mechanical Dentist
Office—Corner of Broad and Pine Streets—up stairs, Nevada City

I would like to inform my friends, and all wishing my services, that I am prepared to attend those favoring me with a call at any hours. Teeth, after having become sensitive by the exposure of the nerve, will be filled without causing pain. . . .

I am permanently located in this city. Residence on Sacramento Street, third house from Temperance Hall.

Since establishing a practice takes time, Allen decided to also farm on property two to three miles west of the town in what is known today as the Indian Flat area. The site became known as the Chapman Ranch. The property is described in the assessor's rolls of 1862: "Possessory right, title and claim to a certain tract or parcel of land in Township of Nevada, situated on the head of Rush Creek, North of and adjoining the land of Mrs. Webber, containing 70 acres, more or less. Improvements thereon consisting of house, orchard, fencing and fixtures. Personal property consisting of dental instruments and office furniture." Because dental equipment is mentioned, Allen may also have seen patients at this location. Ore was discovered in 1880, but Allen never tried to mine it.

Nellie and Allen were an unlikely match due to the differences in their ages and level of education. Although Nellie had little formal education, she was a quick learner and soon began assisting her husband with his dental work. She sterilized his dental tools, handed them to him as needed, applied iodine after a tooth was removed, and gave pain relievers to the patients. Nellie also gave birth to Sargent Allen on March 20, 1862, and to a second son, Chester Warren, on June 18, 1864, continuing to work with her husband while raising the children.

Nevada City was growing during this period. It now had planked streets, wooden sidewalks, and water service to the houses. These improvements brought in more people, which helped Allen create a successful dental practice. But Allen sometimes had difficulty receiving payment for his services, and he was also a generous man. He cosigned notes for friends that at one point totaled $80,000 and ran into financial difficulty when those notes became due. Although he was advised to declare bankruptcy, he declined, stating, "I went into it with my eyes open and assumed the responsibility. I will therefore pay it to the last cent." He sold off most of his assets, which reduced his debt down to $16,000.

Thinking that he could make more money to pay off his debts, Allen opened a second dental office in Virginia City, Nevada, in 1875. Many of the miners who had been his patients had moved there following the discovery of silver in that state. Allen left Nellie behind in Nevada City to care for his patients who remained there, and she used the dental office that had been created in the parlor of their Sacramento Street home around 1870. Since Nellie felt she had been apprenticing with her husband and now was acting as a dentist while he was away, she decided to make it official. In 1879, dentists were required for the first time to be registered in parts of the West (now California, Nevada, and Arizona). On July 7, 1885, Nellie was listed as No. 59 in the registry of dentists in California, becoming the first female dentist certified in the western states. Imagine her pride when she could list herself as a dentist in the 1900 US census when before she had been noted as "keeping house." With their increased income as two full-fledged dentists with two offices, the Chapmans were able to pay off all of Allen's debts. Allen traveled between the two offices, but when he was in Nevada, Nellie was the only dentist between Sacramento and Donner Lake, a distance of approximately one hundred miles. Nellie acquired the most modern dental equipment available for her practice, including pearl-handled instruments; she wanted to treat her patients "like royalty."

When not busy with dental work, caring for her two children, or tending the three thousand pear and apple trees and large vineyard on their property outside town, Nellie liked to write, especially poetry. She would often read her original work at the Elks Lodge

(Nevada City Benevolent and Protective Order of Elks #518, one of the oldest chapters of that organization in the West), where people thought she gave impressive oral presentations. Nellie also was a prominent member of the local Shakespeare Club, a women's literary club; there were many chapters throughout California in this era and a few remain active today (for example, Placerville in northern California and Pasadena in the south). Nellie was also a competent musician and wrote songs with a family friend, Edward Muller (also known for his successful effort to raise silk worms in California in the 1870s). Some of their musical pieces were published. With her love of literature and music, she must have attended events at the Nevada Theatre, which is touted today as California's oldest existing theater building that still hosts performances. It is designated California Historical Landmark No. 863. Nellie was also an honorary member of the Alpha Upsilon Phi dental sorority of San Francisco and a charter member of the Order of the Eastern Star, an organization for women affiliated with the Freemasons, an organization for men. Allen was a prominent Mason, as well as a Knight Templar (an order of Freemasonry) and a member of the American Legion of Honor.

Allen continued his Virginia City dental practice until 1895, when he was hurt in a "runaway accident" with a horse. He never fully regained his health, even staying in San Diego for a period to see if that milder climate would make a difference. He was inflicted with la grippe (what we call today influenza or the flu) and died on July 8, 1897, at the age of seventy. Nellie sang one of her musical compositions, "Weep Not for Me," at his funeral. The Knights Templar assisted with the funeral rites. Allen is buried at the Pine Grove Cemetery in Nevada City.

In the 1900 records of the Prosperity Oil Company, Nellie is listed as a stockholder, so she continued to diversify her assets after her husband's death. She practiced dentistry in her home on the hill above Deer Creek until she was operated on in San Francisco in July 1905. She was bedridden afterward and died on

April 7, 1906, at the age of fifty-nine. Her death certificate lists exhaustion as the cause, with cancer as a contributing factor. Her obituary in the *Grass Valley Daily Union* focused on her talents as a writer, musical composer, and speaker, and, somewhat as an aside, mentioned that she "practiced dentistry for many years in the city." She was described in that year's publication of *History of the State of California and Biographical Record of the Sierras* as wielding "an uplifting influence in many circles, and [she] was a leader in society by reason of the culture and refinement which distinguished her entire life. A Christian in the truest sense of the word, . . . she made liberality the principle of her life, both in the giving of her time and means, counting nothing lost that meant the uplifting of a needy one. Not only was her death a sad blow to her family and immediate friends, but was felt as a public loss to her home town."

"Weep Not for Me," the musical composition Nellie sang at her husband's funeral, was also sung at her funeral. And like her husband, Nellie is buried in the Pine Grove Cemetery. The house where she practiced dentistry in Nevada City still stands and remains in the family. Both of the Chapman sons chose to also become dentists. After attending Cooper Medical College of San Francisco, Sargent Allen practiced in Virginia City with his father and took over his practice when Allen returned to California. After studying at the dental school at the University of California in San Francisco and graduating from the College of Dental Surgery of the University of Pennsylvania in 1891, Chester Warren opened a dental practice in Nevada City. His office was in the IOOF (Independent Order of Odd Fellows) building on Broad Street and his name was written in gold letters on one of the windows. Like his parents, he was active in community affairs. He served on the Nevada City Council and was mayor from 1904 to 1906. In 1901, he had been chosen to chair the Donner Monument Committee. The Donner Party, immigrants to California who were trapped by snow when crossing the Sierra Nevada in 1846–1847, are infamous for having resorted to cannibalism to survive the winter. It was

Chester's suggestion that the height of the monument pedestal be the same as the level of the snow (twenty-two and a half feet) at the party's winter encampment. The monument, which is located about 50 miles east of Nevada City at the spot where the Donner Party spent the winter, was dedicated June 5, 1918. At the time of Chester's death in May 1956 (at age ninety-one), he was the oldest practicing dentist in the country. Establishing records in the field of dentistry seems to have run in this family.

Nellie paved the way for women dentists in California, but there are still far more male dentists than female ones in the state today. While the number of female students in dental schools is increasing, in 2012 only 30 percent of practicing California dentists were women, up only 1 percent from 2008. Four years later, in April 2016, the total again had risen by only 1 percent. As a trailblazer in the medical field, Nellie had to fight skepticism from male colleagues. One extremely vocal opponent was Dr. Alfred E. Regensburger, a dermatologist practicing in San Francisco. He made his feelings about women doctors and dentists clear in an address to the California State Medical Society in 1875: "If we ignore them and downplay their efforts they will be forced to abandon the idea of being part of medicine." But because Nellie persevered, her story was included as part of an exhibit at the Women's Museum of California in San Diego from June 2013 to December 2014. Today, her dental chair, tools, and books are displayed at the School of Dentistry at the University of California in San Francisco. Nellie remains an inspiration for all women seeking to enter professions where men still outnumber women.

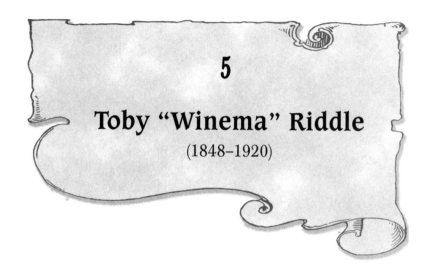

5

Toby "Winema" Riddle

(1848–1920)

PEACEMAKER BY ANY NAME

Toby knew this wasn't a good idea, but the white men wouldn't listen. They thought she was being a foolish Modoc woman. US Army General Edward Richard Sprigg Canby and Reverend Eleazar Cady Thomas, a Methodist minister from Petaluma, believed Toby was just overreacting to the possible danger. Canby assured the others in the group that the Modocs would "*dare not* molest us because his troops commanded the situation." Thomas drew on his faith, stating "that where God called him to go, *he would go*." They were so sure they were right that they even planned to go unarmed to the meeting Toby was so worried about. Alfred Benjamin Meacham (who usually went by A. B.) had once been the superintendent of Indian Affairs in Oregon. He knew Toby and considered her to be a truthful person, and although he trusted her judgment, he also believed it was his duty to attend because he had been named the chairman of the group. Indian Agent Leroy S. Dyar sided with Meacham and also agreed to go, even though he went reluctantly.

Toby Riddle, standing at center, with four other Modoc women. Frank Riddle at back right.
–Photographed by US Army photographer Eadweard Muybridge, circa 1872–1873; US National Archives

These men constituted an official government committee–the Indian Peace Commission, appointed in 1873 by President Ulysses S. Grant to enact the 1868 Peace Policy with tribes. The government felt it had reasoned with the Modocs before and could do the same with Chief Kintpuash (also recorded as Kientpoos). The tribe had been required to leave their native lands in northern California and move onto a reservation in Oregon in 1864, when a leader named Old Schonchin signed a treaty with the government. They had to share the reservation with the Klamath tribe. Although the two tribes had once been united (the word Modoc is said to mean "southern people" in the Klamath language), now they were bitter enemies, and because the Modocs had been moved to Klamath land, the Klamath tribe felt superior. Modoc leaders appealed to government officials to move one of the tribes, but their appeal was unsuccessful. Some Modocs left the reservation in 1865 hoping to get their own reservation in their old homeland. Their presence unnerved the white settlers, so Chief Kintpuash and his people were persuaded to return to the Klamath Reservation in 1869. In April 1870, Chief Kintpuash again led many of his tribe back to their homeland at Lost River, just north of Tule Lake. Since their traditional means of existence had effectively been destroyed by white settlers, the Modoc men found jobs handling livestock on ranches and some of the women found husbands in Yreka. But two years later, in 1872, President Grant ordered the return of all Modocs to the reservation. Although the military wanted to use force against the tribe, they allowed Toby to act as interpreter and hopefully be a peacemaker because she was related to the chief. Toby reasoned that "No peace can be made as long as soldiers are near. Let me speak with my cousin and see what can be done without war."

Finally, on a cold winter day in 1873, Chief Kintpuash agreed that if the Modoc people could be placed at a certain location on the Klamath Reservation (now known as Modoc Point), they would return. The members of the Indian Peace Commission were thrilled with their accomplishment and started praising each other and patting each other on the back. Their boisterous actions upset the chief, and his braves drew their weapons. Only through Toby's efforts was no one hurt. The agreement held together for a while, but tensions quickly escalated again as nothing was done to honor the Modocs' request for months.

Chief Kintpuash was better known as Captain Jack because he loved and wore a blue jacket with brass buttons and military insignias. He asked Toby to meet with him the day before the upcoming meeting with the Indian Peace Commission. Traveling to the meeting under a flag of truce, Toby thought of her young son. Would the Modoc people see her as a traitor and kill her? She was right to be concerned. Upon her arrival, a dozen pistols were pointed at her. Climbing up on a rock so that all could see, she put her hand on her own gun and shouted, "I am a Modoc myself. I am here to talk peace. Shoot me if you dare, but I will never betray you."

After enduring several hours of mockery and cruel remarks by her people because she worked for the government that had broken so many promises to them, she managed to get Captain Jack to agree to attend the peace summit the next day. He would bring along five unarmed warriors. Something in his manner, however, made Toby extremely uneasy. She knew that while her cousin preferred to work peacefully with the government, other Modocs were ready for a fight, and he had to abide by the will of his people if he wanted to remain their leader. Toby's intuition was right. As she was leaving the Modoc camp, one of Captain Jack's followers warned her that they were plotting to kill the peace commissioners. The Modocs mistakenly believed that the Americans would leave if their leaders were killed; with the leaders gone, the tribe could stay where it wanted to live.

It was April 11, 1873, Good Friday—a day of renewal and rebirth and a beautiful spring day. Bright pink and orange wildflowers dotted areas of the landscape and contrasted sharply with the grim mood of the men preparing to meet Captain Jack. Just before leaving for the meeting, Meacham wrote a quick note to his wife: "You may be a widow tonight; you shall not be a coward's wife. I go to save my honor. . . . The chances are all against us. I have done my best to prevent this meeting."

At about 11 a.m., Toby and her husband, Frank, started off with the commissioners. Their son shouted to his parents, "If the Modocs kill you, I will avenge you if it takes a lifetime." Under a flag of truce, the group headed toward Captain Jack and the other five warriors (Schonchin John [brother of Old Schonchin], Black

Jim, Ellen's Man George, Shacknasty Jim, and Hooker Jim). Two other braves, Boston Charley and Bogus Charley, went out with the peace commissioners because they had spent the night with the Riddles. After a round of cigars at the meeting tent, the negotiations began. Captain Jack requested that the soldiers be removed from around the village. He also asked for a separate reservation for his people. The commissioners denied his requests.

At this point Captain Jack had had enough. Reportedly he said, "*Ut wih kutt*," (meaning "All ready" or "Let's do it"), and the Modocs pulled out guns. Quickly assessing the situation, Toby's husband, Frank, and Indian Agent Dyar bolted away on foot and escaped, although they were followed and shot at by Black Jim and Hooker Jim. Captain Jack raised his revolver at General Canby. It misfired. Canby was so shocked at what was occurring that he seemed paralyzed. Captain Jack cocked the gun again and shot Canby in the face. The other braves starting shooting. Reverend Thomas was killed by Boston Charley, and Canby and Thomas were scalped. Meacham was shot several times and fell to the ground unconscious. When Toby saw that a brave was preparing to scalp him, she shouted that the soldiers were coming and all the warriors fled. Captain Jack donned Canby's coat before heading south to the lava beds on the south shore of Tule Lake. The lava beds are known today as Captain Jack's Stronghold. Toby rode quickly to find the government troops, share the fateful events of the day, and get help for Meacham, who was barely alive. The cold-blooded murder of General Canby, who was touted as a Civil War hero in the news stories about this event, pushed the US Army to launch a major attack against Captain Jack and the Modocs. Toby had done all she could to help her people live in peace.

———— • • • ————

Traditionally, Modoc children were not given a name until they were one year old. At that age, Toby was named *Kaitchkona*. She was born at a location close to the Link River (near the present-day city of Klamath Falls, Oregon) in September 1848. Her mother died in childbirth, so she was raised by her father, Secot, and an older sister and brother. She loved listening to the Modoc tribal elders as they told stories of her heritage. Since she was strong and athletic, her father took her on grizzly bear hunts, and he taught her Modoc traditions. Unlike other children, she showed no fear of the sacred places of the tribe nor observed taboos. This earned her the nickname *Nonooktowa*, which translates loosely as "Strange Child." Her interest in activities considered masculine probably also contributed to this sobriquet (nickname). She thrived and grew up quickly in this environment. One day while she was canoeing on a lake with other children, their canoe was pulled into a powerful current. Parents watching from the shore wailed in fear; they were sure their children were about to die. Kaitchkona stood up and ably steered the canoe around the huge boulders that stood in its path and directed the boat to a calm spot in the lake. All were safe. After this, a more respectful nickname emerged. The adults started calling her *Kaitchkona Winema*, "The Little Woman Chief."

Winema saw her first white person when she was a child. A man became lost on his way north, and when she and her father found him, he was helpless and starving. They took him back to the Modoc village, and she nursed him back to health. It was from him that Winema learned about the great cities in the eastern United States. She asked many questions in order to learn how his culture compared to hers.

In the course of their existence, the Modoc people never numbered more than eight hundred men, women, and children, and they lived in separate groups that loosely followed one leader. Occasionally, members of the Modoc tribe would visit the miners working around the town of Yreka, which was established in 1851 (the present county seat of Siskiyou County, California). On one of these trips as a teenager, Winema met Tazewell Francis Riddle (as listed in the 1867 Voter Registration Register for Siskiyou County). Better known as Frank, he was a white settler who had emigrated from Kentucky to California in 1850 for the Gold Rush. Although he was engaged to a woman in his home state, he felt, in his words, "a goneness in my heart" for the Indian girl with reddish-brown hair. He and Winema were married a few weeks after they met in 1862. In marrying Frank, Winema defied both Modoc tradition and her father, who had already selected a husband for her. Winema also acquired another name. Following her marriage she became known as Toby (sometimes spelled Tobey) Riddle, not only to the white community but also to her native people.

Frank and Toby settled on a ranch in the Lost River area, where the Modoc tribe lived, and Toby quickly adapted to her life as a miner's wife. Frank and Toby would visit her family during the dry season, when mining became difficult. Frank was initially rejected by Toby's relatives and tribe, but he was determined to change their feelings about him. He fulfilled the traditional obligations of a Modoc groom by giving horses to his new father-in-law, and he went hunting and fishing with Toby's father and brother. Eventually, Frank was accepted into the family. Toby bore a son named *Charka* ("Handsome One") on November 30, 1863.

Tension escalated between the Modocs and the miners, farmers, settlers, and soldiers who kept moving into their traditional homeland. Toby was often called upon to act as peacemaker between the whites and Native Americans because she could speak both English and the Modoc language (*Lutuami*). Once the Modocs were forcibly removed from California and placed on reservation land in Oregon, however, her job became much harder. Many Modocs fled the reservation and resisted the efforts of the government forces trying to convince them to return. Toby tried to prevent an all-out war and was successful until that fateful day in April 1873. Newspapers across the country reported the killings and set the country against the Modocs. The *Memphis Daily Appeal* noted, "The assassination of General Canby . . . will exasperate the country against the Indians as never before." Others called the Modocs "wild beasts," and several newspapers demanded the extermination of the entire tribe.

What followed is known today as the Modoc War or the Lava Beds War. Captain Jack and the Modocs were able to defend themselves from multiple cavalry attacks in the ridges, crevices, and caves of the lava field, which they called "The Land of Burnt-Out Fires." On April 17, 1873, the troops captured Captain Jack's Stronghold but found it empty. During the previous night the women, children, and some of the men had quietly withdrawn through a lava flow and headed south while other braves provided a diversion. Various skirmishes followed, including one in which many soldiers were killed in a surprise attack. By mid-May, the Modocs had broken into smaller groups, and one band of fighters had surrendered. That group agreed to help the soldiers capture Captain Jack and the people with him. Captain Jack surrendered on June 1, 1873. In the final US Army report about the event, it was noted that Captain Jack said he gave up because his "legs had given out" from all of his efforts to evade the soldiers.

Captain Jack and five other warriors (Schonchin John, Black Jim, Boston Charley, Barncho, and Sloluck) were tried for the murders of Canby and Thomas. Barncho and Sloluck were boys who had brought guns to the braves at the meeting. Toby testified at the military trial, which began July 5, 1873, and attempted to explain what motivated the Modocs to take such a drastic action that April day. A frail but recovered A. B. Meacham also attended and was shocked that the Modocs had not been provided legal counsel. But the support efforts of both Toby and Meacham were futile; all of the defendants were found guilty of the following:

Charge 1: Murder, in violation of the laws of war

Specification 1: Murder of General Canby

Specification 2: Murder of Reverend Thomas

Charge 2: Assault, with intent to kill, in violation of the laws of war

Specification 1: The attack on A. B. Meacham

Specification 2: The attack on Agent Dyar

The sentence was death. Captain Jack and the three others directly involved in the killings were hung on October 3, 1873. The sentences of the two boys were reduced to life imprisonment at the military prison on Alcatraz Island in San Francisco Bay. The rest of the Modoc Indians who were found with Captain Jack (thirty-nine men, fifty-four women, and sixty children) were considered prisoners of war and were sent by rail in cattle cars to the Quapaw Agency in the northeastern corner of Indian Territory (now Oklahoma). The other braves who participated in the attack on the commissioners were pardoned because they assisted the soldiers in locating Captain Jack. The Modocs who had stayed on the reservation were not affected.

The Modoc War was costly, in terms of both money and lives. It is estimated to have cost the United States over $400,000. If the government had purchased the land the Modoc people requested for a separate reservation, it could have been acquired for around $20,000 and the entire problem would have been resolved. To help the government officials understand why the war was so expensive, the US Army hired photographer Eadweard Muybridge to take pictures of the harsh terrain where battles had taken place. During the fighting, it is estimated that sixty Modoc braves waged war against one thousand soldiers. In the end, fifty-three US soldiers, seventeen civilians, and fifteen Modoc warriors lost their lives. A. B. Meacham survived his attack because of Toby's actions, and he later stated, "Of the several characters developed by the Modoc Indian War of 1873, none stands out with more claim to an honorable place in history than Wi-ne-ma, the woman-chief."

Meacham published two accounts of the events that occurred in the Modoc War. *Wigwam and War-Path; or, The Royal Chief in Chains*, a history of the war, was published in 1875. *Wi-ne-ma (the Woman Chief) and Her People*, published in 1876, was dedicated to Toby (under her native name): "This book is written with the avowed purpose of doing honor to the heroic Wi-ne-ma who at the peril of her life sought to save the ill fated peace commission to the Modoc Indians in 1873. The woman to whom the writer is indebted, under God, for saving his life."

Meacham also wrote a lecture-play, *The Tragedy of the Lava Beds*, in 1883. He organized a theatrical group that included Toby, Frank, and their son, now known as Jefferson C. Davis Riddle to honor US Army General Jefferson C. Davis, who ended the Modoc War. Meacham talked while the others acted out scenes. After a positive

Winema (Toby Riddle) and son. –Photographed by Louis Heller,
Library of Congress Prints and Photographs Division, Washington DC

start in Sacramento, the show toured for several years in the East. As noted in the *Sacramento Record,* at the end of each performance "Mr. Meacham paid a glowing tribute to the devotion, truth, and sagacity of Toby Riddle, and declared her a heroine of the highest order." This made Toby a celebrity. President Grant even honored her with a parade when the show passed through Washington DC.

Other people profited from Toby's wartime service without her consent. In 1873, T. C. Harbaugh, under the pen name (pseudonym, or fictitious name) Captain Charles Howard, wrote a dime novel titled *The Squaw Spy; or, the Rangers of the Lava-Beds.* Dime novels were inexpensive melodramatic stories popular in the United States at that time. The main character in Howard's novel is a woman who provides intelligence to the army about the intentions of the Modocs. While real people, such as Captain Jack, are included, Toby is not named.

While the lecture tour was a publicity success, it did not earn the Riddles much money. Toby, Frank, and Jeff returned to Oregon after the tour ended. Tourists would stop by their home in Yainax Butte, on the Klamath Reservation, and take Toby's picture for a fee. Representative Binger Hermann introduced a bill in the US Congress on her behalf, and by a special act of Congress, pension certificate number 565101 was issued to "Winemah Riddell [*sic*]" on February 25, 1891. The act noted that the pension "at the rate of twenty-five dollars per month" was granted "for service rendered Commission to the Modoc Indians." This was a reward for her years of work in trying to keep the peace. Toby donated this money to her tribe. When Jane Stanford, the widow of railroad industrialist and former California governor Leland Stanford, learned of her story and service to the government in 1895, she built Toby a house and pledged to support her family for the rest of her life.

Frank died on February 21, 1906, and is buried in Chief Schonchin Cemetery in Klamath County, Oregon. A memorial to him reads:

In Memory of Frank Tazewell Riddle, Native of Kentucky

Miner, Rancher, Frontiersman,

Guide and Interpreter during the Modoc War 1872–1873

Beloved Husband of Winema

Dedicated by Klamath County Historical Society

October 1985

That same year, the Modoc people who had been forced to move to Oklahoma were allowed to return to the reservation in Oregon if they wanted to relocate.

In 1914, Jefferson C. Davis Riddle published the book *Indian History of the Modoc War*. He wanted to give the native view of the Modoc War; as a ten-year-old he had witnessed the conflict firsthand. He followed his mother's lead of caring for the Modoc people when he became a councilman and judge for tribal members who had remained in Oregon.

Toby fell victim to the great influenza epidemic that lasted from 1918 to 1920; she died on February 17, 1920, and is buried in Chief Schonchin Cemetery. The Winema Chapter of the Daughters of the American Revolution, organized in Corvallis, Oregon, on December 28, 1920, was mentioned in an inscription placed on a memorial to her in 1932:

In Memory of Winema, Modoc Heroine Interpreter for
Peace Commission Pensioned by Congress for
Courageous and Loyal Service Modoc War 1872–1873

Presented by Winema Chapter

Placed by Eulaona Chapter

Daughters of the American Revolution

May 30, 1932

In 1954, the Klamath Termination Act ended government oversight of the inhabitants of the Klamath Reservation. Some land was sold, and the profits were distributed among the former residents of the reservation. Most of the land was incorporated into the Winema National Forest, named in Toby's honor in 1961. The Modoc and Klamath people did regain federal recognition as tribes, however. The descendants of the Modoc people who were forcibly relocated to Oklahoma are today known as the Modoc Tribe of Oklahoma. The descendants of the Modocs who never left the Klamath Reservation or who returned to Oregon in 1906 are now one of the tribes recognized collectively as the Klamath Tribes. Their former reservation land, however, remains public property. Lava Beds National Monument was created on November 21, 1925. Run by the National Park Service, it encompasses over forty-six thousand acres and includes the area where the Modoc War was fought. In 2002, the Fremont and Winema National Forests merged as the Fremont-Winema National Forest.

The name Winema is prominent in Siskiyou County, California. The Winema School District was formed in 1929. Although it became part of the Tulelake School District in 1954, the original school building is still in use as a storage facility. Businesses and farms still identify themselves by the name today, and there is also a Winema Cemetery.

The name Winema is also prominent in Oregon. The *Winema* was the largest steamboat ever to operate on Upper Klamath Lake in that state. The name was picked through a contest and the winner suggested the name to honor Toby. The steamer ran from 1905 to 1919 but was destroyed by fire in the 1920s. Winema School, originally named the Chemeketa Alternative High program at Chemeketa Community College, started in the early 1980s in Salem, Oregon. Its new name reflects its location at Winema Place on the college campus. Winema Beach is located in Cloverdale.

Although Toby was honored and is best known for her role as a peacemaker, she also learned to weave baskets—a traditional skill at which the Modocs excelled. On December 7, 1954, the *Reno Evening Gazette* reported that a basket made by Toby was being returned to Oregon after being found in Pennsylvania. Another basket that she made was discussed on a PBS program in 2010. Toby's granddaughter, who lives in Klamath Falls, helped authenticate the basket featured on the PBS program *History Detectives*. She also allowed one of Toby's baskets to be displayed at the Klamath County Museum.

Unlike some women who receive recognition for their deeds only posthumously (after they have died), Toby was hailed as courageous during her lifetime. From an early age, she demonstrated determination and spunk. She was curious about how nonnative people lived and aptly navigated between the two worlds by trying to achieve peaceful coexistence for all involved. She was one of the first women in America to be recognized by the federal government for her actions in time of war. This was a worthy accomplishment for any woman, but even more laudable for one who sometimes had her views scoffed at because she was Native American and a woman. Known by both her Modoc and English names, Toby could also be labeled as a Native American statesperson who demonstrated that negotiation is always a worthy step in defusing hostile situations. She was a diplomat in every sense of the word.

6
Elvira Virginia Mugarrieta
(1869–1936)

BREAKING SOCIETY'S RULES

Babe Bean, as Elvira Virginia Mugarrieta was commonly known, enjoyed living on a small houseboat or "ark" on McLeod's Lake in Stockton, California. In the late 1890s, however, this neighborhood was considered to be extremely dangerous by many local citizens because it was "in a desolate and unlighted part of the city." But Babe enjoyed its peace and quiet. No one cared if Babe, who was in her late twenties but looked about eighteen, went out for midnight walks or visited the local saloons to drink lemonade sodas and chew tobacco. Babe always dressed as a man, had short black hair, and carried a gun, so she felt safe interacting with the variety of people in the town. If asked about family, Babe would only comment that they were "one of the best in the land."

After engaging in a written dialogue with a local newspaper, the Stockton *Evening Mail* hired Babe as a reporter because of Babe's "good hand, good English," and correct use of punctuation in all correspondence. Babe claimed to be mute; otherwise "his" feminine voice would reveal his true gender, and thus he had to communicate only through the written word. Babe was assigned

Elvira Mugarrieta as Babe Bean. –Drawing from the Stockton
Evening Mail, October 9, 1897; Stockton Public Library

some hard issues to explore for the newspaper, what today we would call investigative reporting. Babe examined problems in the local mines, the state hospital for the insane, hobo camps, and gambling establishments. One of Babe's articles called for the formation of a group to prevent cruelty to animals, and the headline of another was "Babe Bean's Night Walks: Some of the Things the Ark-Dweller Has Seen After the Good Folks of the Town Have Put on Their Night-Caps and Gone to Bed." Babe also interviewed Stockton residents, including James H. Budd, who served as a member of the US House of Representatives from California's 2nd Congressional District (1883–1885) and as Governor of California from 1895 to 1899. Babe described him as, "Why, just an everyday man is the Governor of California! . . . To me he appeared like a medical gentleman or a lawyer. . . . He struck me as being rather pale, which really made him look even more interesting."

Newspaper readers also learned that on a trip to visit a mine near Angel's Camp, Babe was thrown from a horse-drawn buggy. That event supposedly brought back Babe's ability to speak after being mute for two years. Babe's articles were front-page news for months. Babe became somewhat of a celebrity after stopping a runaway carriage while on a trip to San Francisco. Stockton's Naomi Bachelor Club, reserved for men, gave Babe membership, and sometimes Babe went duck hunting with male friends. It seemed like the ideal situation for Babe.

But the local police had been watching Babe. They were sure the name "Babe" was an alias, and that "he" was really a "she." This really wasn't a secret to the townspeople who read the newspaper and had met Babe. However, things changed radically for Babe on October 2, 1897. The newspaper printed a letter to the editor signed by "The Girls of Stockton." They stated that it was unfair that Babe got to don men's apparel and they couldn't. They offered a warning: "There used to be a law against females dressing like the male human being. Some fine evening, there are going to be about twenty-five young women . . . all dressed in men's clothing and we're going to go to the ark and get Babe Bean and dunk her in McLeod's Lake till she cries, 'Nuff.'"

For Babe was indeed a woman. Two days later, Babe Bean responded to her critics: "Why am I allowed to dress as I choose. Since when pray do you girls take it upon your shoulders to dictate to strangers what they shall or shall not wear in the way of apparel? 'Tis your privilege to dress as you see fit, whether it is after the fashion of Venus or after the fashion of Babe Bean."

The person known as Babe Bean was born as Elvira Virginia Mugarrieta, and while she would occasionally use that name, at other times she would be Jack Bean, Jack Maines, Beebe Beam, or Jack Bee Garland. She once said, "I have been wearing men's clothing off and on for five years . . . for as a man, I can travel freely, feel protected, and find work."

If you walk down any street today, you will probably see both men and women wearing pants. Did you know that this practice only became socially acceptable in the last part of the twentieth century? However, bold women throughout history have discarded their dresses and petticoats and worn men's attire. Using male identities, Deborah Sampson served as a soldier in the American Revolutionary War (disguised as Robert Shurtleff); Sarah Emma Edmonds fought for the North (Union Army) in the Civil War (using the name Franklin Thompson); and Loreta Janeta Velazquez was a Confederate States' Army scout (known as Lieutenant Harry T. Buford) in the Civil War. These women are examples of females who desired the same level of freedom that men enjoyed. By assuming a male persona, they were able to escape the strict regulations placed on women in American society. Elvira Virginia Mugarrieta was one of these women.

———•••———

Elvira's life not only crossed boundaries of gender but also of ethnicity, social class, and geography. Born December 9, 1869, she was the second child of José Marcos Mugarrieta and Eliza Alice

Denny Garland. Elvira's father was a military officer who served fourteen years in the Mexican army before being appointed as San Francisco's first Mexican consul (1857–1863). Her mother was from an upper-class white family. Elvira's maternal grandfather was Rice Garland, a former US Congressman and Louisiana Supreme Court justice. When José and Eliza first arrived in San Francisco, they were welcomed to the city with a lavish reception at the International Hotel. According to the *Daily Alta California* newspaper, it was an evening filled with music, speeches, and champagne. Living in San Francisco's Russian Hill district, Elvira had a life of wealth and status. Being a dutiful daughter, however, was not an easy task for Elvira. She lamented, "How often I wished I could enjoy the liberty that the world sees fit to allow a boy." Her parents sent her to a convent school, hoping religious training would squelch her early rebellious behavior. She later wrote, "I loved my mother with all my heart, but I feared even to talk to her at times, lest my rough manner might offend her. From a tomboy full of ambitions, I was made into a sad and thoughtful woman."

To escape her parents' control, Elvira married her brother's best friend when she was fifteen. The relationship didn't work, however, and she divorced him after a few months. California State Hospital records indicate that Elvira's mother had her admitted to Stockton State Hospital when she was eighteen (May 1888). Elvira's admission papers noted that she was quite intelligent, in good health, and not insane. She went there supposedly because of an opium addiction, but she was released a month later–too soon to truly cure an addict. Was this another attempt by her parents to control her behavior?

Like many other women in the nineteenth century, Elvira discovered that life for a single woman was difficult. Women were expected to marry and live according to the rules made by men. Those who did not were viewed as social failures. Elvira began dressing like a man so she could make her own decisions. She traveled alone and did odd jobs to survive. She didn't talk because her voice would give away her masquerade. In her late teens, Elvira roamed around the Santa Cruz Mountains using the name Jack Bee Garland. After changing her name to Babe Bean, she ended up in Stockton. She might have worn a blue pantsuit with a white silk shirt. Sometimes she added a fedora, a soft felt hat. In 1897, police questioned Babe about the misdemeanor offense of "masquerading in men's clothing." She convinced them that her appearance was not motivated by criminal intent. It was not illegal at this time in California for women to dress like men unless the intent was to defraud others. Elvira must have appreciated how she was treated in Stockton, as she wrote, "I should like to say a word for Stockton men. If the courtesy shown me by the police department and the newspapers alike is a proof of what sons of this pleasant little burg are, then you have more good and generous fellows together here than it has been my lot to meet in any other one place."

Elvira's actions, however, do not imply that she was seeking total equality with the men of the era. She expressed opposition to women's suffrage (the right to vote) in the Stockton *Evening Mail* (September 15, 1897), writing, "No; no new women for me. Some, of course, are sincere, but the majority put me in mind of the old saying, 'Monkey see, monkey do'. . . . The better class of women would not go to the polls, and it is just those that we want."

By obscuring her racial identity, maintaining a younger age than she was, and explaining that she was just a young woman who preferred the freedom offered by wearing men's clothes, Elvira assured the people of Stockton that she was not trying to affect the status quo of society. This is probably why she maintained such goodwill in that town.

In 1898, after the end of the Spanish-American War, the United States wanted to hamper national independence in the Philippines. Elvira desperately wanted to write about the unfolding events. As she noted, "A newspaper woman and the daughter of an army officer, all my ambition and interest and inclination naturally gave me the fever to go to Manila when things were at their liveliest there. . . . My purpose in going to Manila was to see war from the soldier's point of view, through a woman's eyes."

Using the name Jack Bean, she headed for the Philippines on October 5, 1899, taking the job of cabin boy on the troop transport ship *City of Para* to pay her way. Unfortunately, Elvira became sick on the journey due to the administration of a smallpox vaccination and had to confess her true identity to the ship's captain. He put her ashore in Honolulu (Hawaii had been annexed by the United States the previous year). However, the enlisted soldiers did not want to lose her. They collected money to buy her a ticket, but the ship captain still would not allow her back aboard, so the soldiers gave her a uniform, sneaked her back on the ship, and kept her hidden until it left Hawaii.

Using several male aliases to hide her identity in Manila, Elvira worked for almost a year as a Spanish language interpreter, a Red Cross aide, and a war correspondent. She had military approval to travel with the Twenty-Ninth Infantry, so she donned the regular khaki uniform of a soldier with the shoulder straps of a second lieutenant. Today, we would call her an embedded reporter. The soldiers of the unit appreciated her work and contributed $200 to purchase a gold medal for "Jack," and had a ceremony to present it. Before leaving Manila, Elvira memorialized her experience with a tattoo on her arm that included "Manila, 1899," the American flag, crossed guns, and the name Jack. Elvira commented, "I saw war and I lived it." On October 21, 1900, the *San Francisco Examiner* magazine published an article written by Elvira under the name B. Beam titled "My Life as a Soldier." It is ironic that she employed the perspective of a woman "soldier" in this article, since she lived as a male in this time period and did not engage in combat. She drew on her experiences observing the conflict at San Mateo, which was a victory for the revolutionaries, and participating in several marches throughout Luzon, the largest Philippine island.

When Elvira returned to San Francisco, she again dressed as a woman and the 1900 US census lists her as "Elvira" and living with her mother. However, she found that as a woman she was unable to prowl around the city at night to collect materials for her stories as a freelance journalist. She returned to wearing male attire, a risky move because San Francisco had an ordinance that made it illegal to wear the apparel of the opposite sex. Following the great 1906 earthquake and subsequent devastating fires, Elvira served as a male nurse for the American Red Cross, helping the three hundred thousand people who were homeless. She was commended for her efforts by Brigadier-General Frederick Funston, acting commander of the presidio during that disaster who became known as "the man who saved San Francisco."

During World War I, the *Chicago Tribune* (December 30, 1917) published an article titled "Girl Dressed in Men's Togs Held in German Plot." Elvira was accused of being a German spy and arrested at Seal Beach, California. She was released for a lack of evidence that she was the wanted "Madame H." The Espionage Act of 1917 had created strong feelings of paranoia in the country.

Although Elvira had only a small inheritance and a little money earned from writing, she later decided to help those in San Francisco who were living in poverty. The Great Depression, which started in 1929, adversely affected the lives of many people. Realizing that some resented being given charity by a woman, Elvira assumed a male identity, now using the name Jack Bee Garland (drawing upon her mother's maiden name). Dressed in a shabby, blue serge suit, well-worn shoes larger than needed to make her feet look masculine, and a big hat pulled low over the face, she assisted the jobless and homeless. She gave the frightened and hungry people money for coffee or a night's lodging. In contrast to her former desire for fame, Elvira now lived a quiet life, changing rooming houses periodically, and generally escaped being hassled by the police. Affectionately called "Uncle Jack," Elvira continued this selfless behavior for the rest of her life.

After giving away her last dollar in 1936, Elvira went to a friend's house asking for money to get home. A few days later, on

September 19, 1936, people at the corner of Post and Franklin Streets in San Francisco saw a "little old man" with iron-gray hair collapse. This was Elvira, now nearly sixty-seven years old, five feet three inches tall, and weighing 105 pounds. She was taken to a hospital, where she died of peritonitis from an ulcer. Medical authorities performed an autopsy and discovered her masquerade as a man. They also discovered the tattoo that she had acquired in Manila. The authorities were made aware of her female status and began investigating, and not long after, Elvira's family background was revealed. Her older sister, Victoria Mugarrieta Shadburn, who was very prominent in San Francisco society, stated in a newspaper interview that "it's always been a bone of contention—this masquerading of Elvira's. Her insistence on retaining men's clothing always filled me with fear."

Victoria tried to obtain a military burial for Elvira, claiming that she had served as a lieutenant in the US Army. This request was denied since there were no data supporting any real military enlistment or service.

Elvira was buried in the family burial plot in Cypress Lawn Cemetery in Colma, California. Although she had dressed in male clothing much of her life, she was buried in a white satin dress. This Mexican-Anglo woman spent most of her life in the guise of a man and enjoyed activities that would have been socially impossible for most women of any ethnicity in this era to experience, including traveling abroad alone. When American society viewed class status as important and promoted segregation, she boldly interacted with and nurtured others from all walks of life. Elvira once described the way she lived her life as "I have been like driftwood tossed upon the sea of life. But in no other way could I have been contented." Her sister fittingly summed up her life this way: "Suppose you had noble ideas, but the fact you wore skirts, not trousers, was a handicap? Elvira did the only thing she could. She put on pants."

The *Stockton Daily Evening Record* noted her passing:

> Whatever became of Babe Bean?—often asked by old-time Stocktonians when talking in reminiscent mood—has been answered. Jack

71

Bee Garland, 67, philanthropically inclined woman who died in San Francisco this week after successfully fully keeping her disguise as a man for 40 years, is revealed to have been Babe Bean, the eccentric character who lived in an ark on McLeod's Lake in the 1890s and created considerable stir in Stockton long ago.

In 1979, a San Francisco organization created a slide show about her life titled "She Even Chewed Tobacco." The presentation states that in the nineteenth century "a small, but significant group of American women rejected the limitations of the female sphere and claimed the privileges enjoyed by men. . . . They did so by adopting men's clothing, hiding their female identities from most of the world, and passing as men."

This was turned into a short movie in 1983, a fitting tribute for a woman once called a "trouser puzzle." Elvira always recognized that she lived her life outside of the accepted norms of the day and once commented that if she ever wrote her autobiography she would title it *Truth Stranger than Fiction*. We should celebrate that today's society has evolved to a wider acceptance of people's lifestyles and beliefs. It makes us admire even more those who were bold enough to break the norms of their day and live their lives as they chose.

7

Julia Morgan

(1872–1957)

BUILDER OF A CASTLE

The workmen at San Simeon strained to hear the conversation between the frail-looking, scarcely one-hundred-pound, five-foot-tall woman in glasses and the imposing, six-foot-three, well-dressed man with the high voice. They probably guessed correctly that it meant more work for them, but the pair did not acknowledge their presence. A person once noted about the two that "the rest of us could have been a hundred miles away; they didn't pay any attention to anybody. It wouldn't have surprised me at all to see a spark traveling from one skull to the other, back and forth, because those two very different people just clicked."

She was Julia Morgan, the architect designing the ranch on the hill at San Simeon overlooking the California coast near San Luis Obispo. He was William Randolph Hearst, the wealthy owner of a chain of newspapers and magazines who was also prominent in politics. Hearst had proposed in 1919 that Julia design a home for his family on the 240,000-acre, undeveloped property, which the family called "Camp Hill." He told her that he was "tired of camping out and wanted something more comfortable on the Hill"

Portrait of Julia Morgan in 1926. –Julia Morgan Papers, Special Collections and
Archives, Robert E. Kennedy Library, California Polytechnic State University, San Luis Obispo

for his wife and five sons as well as guests. Julia had done work for the Hearst family before, especially for William's mother, Phoebe Apperson Hearst. She knew this commission would be especially challenging because of the isolated location, but Julia thrived on the creativity of architecture. She also felt she might gain more projects from Hearst's vast network of friends in publishing, politics, and Hollywood, so she accepted the commission.

Working with Hearst quickly became problematic. He was used to getting his way and often changed his mind about building designs and placement of artwork from his extensive collection. He once demanded that a large oak tree be rotated so that its branches wouldn't impede people walking by. He ordered a fireplace moved to the other side of a room and, once it was moved, decided he liked it better where it had been, so had it changed back. The Neptune Pool, which held 345,000 gallons of water, was redesigned five times in twelve years. In one report sent to Julia's office in San Francisco by her on-site engineer, Hearst's rapid changes to plans were noted: "Mr. Hearst walked into the office . . . and we spent an hour building and creating new projects. An airport on a hilltop above the fog was one. . . . In thirty minutes he moved the zoo, constructed new bear grottos and divided the present one for cats. He leveled animal hill. . . . We tore down the shop and lowered a dozen oak trees in groups of five. . . . Anyway he laughed a lot and seemed happy."

Hearst recognized this trait in himself and wrote to Julia on March 18, 1920: "All little houses stunning. Please complete before I can think of any more changes." Julia probably found his interference annoying, but when asked about it, she replied that his new ideas were often for the better. It also provided her the opportunity to change her own plans knowing that Hearst couldn't rightfully get upset.

While Hearst had dreams of grandeur for his house, he also had cash-flow issues. At one point, it was estimated that the construction was costing about $30,000 per month. That would equal over $400,000 presently. Keeping track of expenses was one of Julia's nonarchitectural responsibilities. She also hired and fired workers, found specialty workers such as wood carvers, arranged for their food and lodging, and ordered materials and arranged for their transport to the site by ship, rail, and truck. Many times during the construction years, Julia had to telegraph Hearst's secretary, Joseph Willicombe, for funds. She even held off paying herself at times in order to keep the project moving forward.

From 1920 to 1938, on almost every Friday night, Julia took the train south from her office in San Francisco to San Luis Obispo, working on drawings in an upper berth. After dining on oyster stew and coffee in the hotel at the train depot, she would hire a taxi to take her the last fifty-six miles to San Simeon. She worked through the weekend and returned to San Francisco on the Sunday night train, going directly from the station to her office to work on other projects. Julia made this exhausting trip over five hundred times during the construction. Since Julia and Hearst worked together on this project from 1919 to 1947, this unlikely duo must have created a solid working relationship somehow. Drawing upon the Spanish Revival style of architecture made popular by the 1915 Panama-California Exposition in San Diego, Hearst formally called his home La Cuesta Encantada (The Enchanted Hill). It was definitely Julia Morgan who made it that way.

———•••———

Julia Morgan was born in San Francisco, California, on January 20, 1872, and it quickly became apparent to her parents, Charles and Eliza, that she was a tomboy. While other little girls from financially secure, upper-middle-class families in the late nineteenth century played with dolls and had tea parties, Julia preferred to chase her older brother, Parmelee, and jump on the trampoline in her family's barn at the home in Oakland where they moved in 1874. Nicknamed Dudu (from her brother's effort to say Julia), she and her sister, Emma (born in 1874), did take dancing and music lessons. Thanks to money provided by her mother's father, the family traveled by transcontinental railroad to New York so that each grandchild could be christened in the time-honored family church. Julia attended Riverside Grammar School and Oakland High School. Her father strongly believed in education for daughters as well as sons and Julia liked to learn. Although her mother hoped she would marry and stop studying so hard, Julia considered both medicine and music as career options before deciding on architecture. When Julia was growing up, her father used to take the family (which also included Avery, born in 1876, and Gardner Buckley, born in 1880) into San Francisco on weekends to see construction sites. To Julia, buildings were like huge puzzles; she wanted to know how to get all of the pieces to fit together. One of her cousins, Pierre LeBrun, was an architect in New York City. He directed the construction of the Metropolitan Life Insurance Tower, one of the first skyscrapers in Manhattan. Julia's goal was to become an architect like Pierre.

After graduating from high school in 1890, Julia entered the University of California at Berkeley. She studied civil engineering because the school didn't offer classes in architectural design. Julia was the only woman in the program at that time. One of her instructors, Bernard Maybeck, had studied at the École des Beaux-Arts in Paris, France, which was considered the best school of architecture in the world. Julia longed to go there, too, but the school did not accept female students.

Julia graduated from college in 1894 and went to work for Maybeck. She also took drawing classes at the Mark Hopkins School of Art Instruction (now called the San Francisco Art Institute). Maybeck had stayed in contact with other students from the École des Beaux-Arts and was told that the school was considering allowing women into its program. Julia did not wait for confirmation. She packed her trunk, took a train to the East Coast, and boarded a steamship to France, arriving in Paris in June 1896. But the rumor about the school changing its admission policy was not true; Julia was not permitted to take the entrance examination.

But she was not disheartened. She prepared for the exam anyway by working in the studios of two architects who taught at the school: Marcel deMonclos and, later, Benjamin Chaussemiche. She loved Paris. On weekends, she would explore magnificent buildings such as Versailles, the palace of French King Louis XIV, and Gothic cathedrals such as Notre Dame and Sainte Chapelle. So much wonderful architecture to see! She sketched many of the things she saw. She also had to learn to speak and write in French.

A year passed. Although she had to move to a cheaper apartment and sometimes skip eating so she could buy books about architecture, Julia did not give up. Finally, in October 1897, she was allowed to take the entrance exam. She ranked 47th out of 376 applicants, but the school admitted only thirty students a year. She tried again, also unsuccessfully, in April 1898. She was finally accepted into the program in November 1898, when she was twenty-six years old. The *San Francisco Examiner* touted her achievement: "Another California girl is added to the long list of those who have won honor for themselves and for their state abroad. The latest on the list is Miss Julia Morgan, who has just successfully passed the entrance examinations for the École des Beaux-Arts, department of Architecture. The honor is all the more marked that Miss Morgan is the first woman in the world to be admitted to this special department."

Julia worked hard. It usually took students six years to complete the program, but Julia finished in slightly more than three. According to school regulations, she had to complete her studies by the age of thirty. Her final project, which was to design a theater in a palace, won her a first-place award. Graduating in February 1902, she became the first woman to receive a certificate in architecture from the École des Beaux-Arts.

After six years in France, Julia was eager to get back to the United States. Her New York friends wanted her to stay in the city, but Julia missed California. She worked for over a year from her family home in Oakland. She assisted John Galen Howard, the architect for the University of California at Berkeley campus, in constructing additions to that site. These included the Greek Theater, the first classical, open-air theater in the country, built to hold six thousand people. When President Theodore Roosevelt came to give the graduation address in May 1903, Julia had to design banners to cover the still-wet concrete on the back wall.

In 1904, after passing the test for state certification, Julia opened her own studio at 456 Montgomery Street in San Francisco as California's first licensed woman architect. When the 1906 earthquake totally destroyed this office, she moved to the Merchants Exchange Building on California Street, a high-rise building that did not crumble on the shaking earth (and is still in use today). Julia found herself swamped with post-earthquake commission requests. One of her early commissions had been a bell tower called El Campanil for Mills College in Oakland, California, across the bay eastward from San Francisco. In spite of the massive weight of ten bronze bells weighing a total of ten thousand pounds, the tower had withstood the earthquake along with every other building she had designed. Her understanding of how to effectively use reinforced concrete was the key factor in this accomplishment. Julia did post-earthquake repair on the six-hundred-room Fairmont Hotel in San Francisco. It was so badly damaged that some thought it should just be razed. Julia worked long hours with rats jumping over her feet in her office in a construction shed at the site. She met the owner's goal of having the hotel operational again on the one-year anniversary of the earthquake (April 18, 1907). When asked by a news reporter why she had restored the hotel rather than tearing it down as others had recommended, she said, "No one asked me—they just said 'Fix it.'" Julia also helped many people repair or rebuild their homes after the devastating earthquake, using her philosophy of building a structure that fit into its surrounding environment and pleased the client.

The early part of the twentieth century saw women banding to-gether to support different causes. The movements for temperance (abstaining from alcoholic beverages) and suffrage (gaining the right to vote) allowed women to meet and support each other. Many clubs were formed by women for recreational, educational, and civic purposes. Consequently, many of Julia's commissions were for women's organizations, totaling over one hundred buildings by the end of her career. Examples of these are the buildings for the Young Women's Christian Association (YWCA) in Oakland (1913) and San Jose (1915), the YWCA Building at the Panama-Pacific International Exposition in San Francisco (1915), the Sausalito Women's Club (1916), the San Francisco Nurses' Association building (1925), and the Oakland Women's City Club (1929). Her largest project of this kind was Asilomar, the YWCA national conference center located in Pacific Grove, California, which she started in 1913. For this project she employed the Arts and Crafts style of architecture, which includes horizontal lines that blend into the landscape and wood shingles, exposed support beams, and materials such as California redwood left natural to create earth tones. From massive stone entrance gates, a chapel, dining hall, administration building, and many room accommodations for visitors, Julia continued adding features to Asilomar through 1928. This facility is now known as the Asilomar State Beach and Conference Grounds State Park and is run by the California Department of Parks and Recreation. Thirteen of the Morgan buildings still stand and are in use. Ironically, this locale is California's second-most-popular state park, right after another of her designs, the one at San Simeon now known as Hearst Castle.

Julia had done over 450 projects by the time she met William Randolph Hearst in 1919 and became involved with the construction at the San Simeon site, but that was the only project for which she also created buildings for a zoo. In what was once the largest private zoo in the world, Hearst had lions, polar bears, leopards, and giraffes housed in pens; zebras, yaks, and kangaroos roamed free. Signs posted along the road up to the house offered a warning: "Animals have the right of way." The author of the

Julia Morgan with Marianne the elephant around 1929. –Julia Morgan Papers, Special Collections and Archives, Robert E. Kennedy Library, California Polytechnic State University, San Luis Obispo

children's picture book *Madeline*, Ludwig Bemelmans, wrote about driving up the hill: "There were wandering herds of zebra, of yaks, of water buffalo, springbok, and deer of every description. . . . The animals were used to cars, and as I went on, the heads of a dozen bison appeared a few feet from the windshield. It is strangely simple, like turning the pages of a children's book."

The wild animals also caused Julia more work. She wrote to Hearst in October 1925 about some reindeer requiring "Iceland moss and careful feeding and watching until used to new food."

She had to house the reindeer temporarily on the tennis courts. Although most of the animals were donated to various zoos starting in 1937, some of the offspring of others (such as deer and zebras) still remain on-site today.

When work on San Simeon stopped, Hearst's original idea of a little bungalow had 165 rooms located between the main house, called Casa Grande, and the three guest cottages, Casa Del Sol (faces west to view the sunset), Casa Del Monte (faces north to the Santa Lucia mountain range), and Casa Del Mar (faces south toward the sea). There were also 127 acres of gardens, which included over one thousand rosebushes, a flower Hearst enjoyed; two pools (indoor and outdoor); two libraries; and facilities for horseback riding, bowling, playing billiards, and fishing, as well as a private movie theater, where he showed films from his own movie studio, Cosmopolitan Productions.

Hearst entertained the elite of the 1920s and 1930s from Hollywood and around the world. Winston Churchill, who became prime minister of Great Britain in 1940, was a guest in September 1929. US Presidents Calvin Coolidge and Franklin Delano Roosevelt visited, as did millionaire Howard Hughes and flying legends Amelia Earhart and Charles Lindbergh. Charlie Chaplin was a frequent Hollywood visitor, and film star Cary Grant was reported to have stayed thirty-four times, asking to be in a different guest room for each visit. Guests entertained themselves during the day, but all were expected at the evening meal with Hearst. While Hearst did allow alcoholic beverages, he did not permit drunkenness or profanity. Guests who broke his rules soon found their bags packed and travel plans arranged.

When Julia was on-site, she ate dinner with Hearst and his guests. Adela Rogers St. Johns, who knew Hearst from when she worked as a reporter for his newspaper, the *San Francisco Examiner*, and was a frequent house guest, once described Julia as "a double-take of unexpectedness. For she was a small, skinny, self-effacing lady . . . graying hair was held in a small knob at the back of her head by bone pins. . . . At dinner . . . , Miss Morgan, in a blue foulard dress with white daisies, was like a small neat bantam hen among birds of paradise."

Julia did many other projects with Hearst in addition to San Simeon. She produced designs for buildings at Wyntoon, supposedly named after the Wintu, a local Indian tribe that had previously lived in the same area near Mount Shasta in northern California. Drawing upon its isolated location on fifty thousand acres of forest, she oversaw the construction of a "Bavarian village," primarily from 1933 to 1938, on the McCloud River nestled among the huge ponderosa pines. Three-story guesthouses with fairy-tale names such as Cinderella House, Fairy House, and Bear House were placed around an open courtyard; a Swiss painter created scenes from Grimm's fairy tales on the outside of two of the houses. While the San Simeon estate was created to host thirty to fifty guests, Wyntoon was planned to accommodate up to one hundred people for a weekend. The Hearst family has retained Wyntoon for its personal use.

Julia also completed Jolon, or the Milpitas Ranch House, in 1932. It was built in Mission Revival style about twenty-three miles north of San Simeon near the Mission of San Antonio de Padua (California's third Spanish mission). Hearst envisioned his San Simeon guests riding horses to this lodge and spending the night in an early California environment. It must have looked authentic, as Julia once wrote to Hearst: "Many tourists are mistaking the new buildings for the Mission—it was really quite amusing last visit." In December 1940, Hearst sold this building and over 150,000 acres of the San Simeon property to the US government. Today the building is located inside the US Army's Hunter-Liggett Military Reservation and operates as a hotel called the Hacienda. The building was placed on the National Register of Historic Places in 1977. In addition, Julia drew plans for some of Hearst's projects that were never built, including the Babicora Hacienda (1943), Hearst's rancho in Mexico, and the Museum for Medieval Arts in San Francisco's Golden Gate Park (1941).

Hearst left his San Simeon property in 1947 due to a heart condition that needed medical care unavailable in the area. He never lived there again, and he died in Beverly Hills, California, in 1951. In 1957, the Hearst Corporation donated San Simeon to the State of California, which opened it up to the public as a museum. The Hearst San Simeon Estate was placed on the National Register of Historic Places in 1972 and was named a National (1976) and State (1958) Historical Landmark. Over a million people visit the property every year, and they can select from a variety of tours to see everything that Julia orchestrated in what is now more commonly known as Hearst Castle.

Julia spent more than half of her forty-seven-year career working on San Simeon. In total, she designed almost eight hundred buildings, probably because her motto was "Never turn down a job because you think it's too small; you don't know where it can lead." These included hotels, schools, banks, hospitals, churches, and private residences. Most were in California, but she also took commissions in Hawaii and the Midwest. She retired in the early 1950s and led a reclusive life in San Francisco. As a child, she had an inner ear problem with her mastoid gland after a bout with scarlet fever (a contagious childhood disease). In 1932, she underwent surgery trying to solve this issue. An error affected the nerves in her face, which became partially paralyzed. Her inner ear was totally removed, causing her to often feel unbalanced and dizzy. Her health also must have been weakened by her grueling work schedule for so many years. As one of her staff commented, "All her life was work—morning, day, and night."

Julia died on February 2, 1957, at the age of eighty-five. Although there are many references to her destroying all of her work before she died, many of her architectural designs, drawings, sketchbooks, photographs, letters, project files, and other papers (both personal and professional) are housed at the California Polytechnic State University in San Luis Obispo. She is buried in Mountain View Cemetery in Oakland, with other members of her family.

In a male-dominated profession, Julia Morgan became one of the most prolific architects in American history. Her trailblazing career opened the field of architecture to American women. Not only did she demonstrate by example that a woman could be an architect, but she also helped expand the field by hiring and training other women as artists, drafters, and architects for her projects. She did not write about her work professionally, however, and turned down most requests for interviews, which may be the reason that her achievements were largely unrecognized for many years. As one of her employees once stated, "Julia Morgan believed that architecture is a form of art, not an art of words. She was not given to talking, writing, or gesturing about her profession."

In June 1929, her alma mater, the University of California at Berkeley, awarded her an honorary doctorate. It was one of the few awards she accepted. The degree states:

> Distinguished alumna of the University of California; Artist and Engineer; Designer of simple dwellings and stately homes, of great buildings nobly planned to further the centralized activities of her fellow citizens; Architect in whose works harmony and admirable proportions bring pleasure to the eye and peace to the mind.

The Julia Morgan School for Girls is a private middle school (grades 6–8) located in a building Julia designed in 1924 on the Mills College campus in Oakland. It opened in 1999 and remains a fully accredited institution under the guidelines of the California Association of Independent Schools. Julia was selected as the school's namesake, according to the school's mission and history statement, because of her ties to the area and her "ability to overcome great obstacles and break barriers for women in the combined fields of art and technology [which] makes her life and spirit an invaluable inspiration."

The State of California recognized Julia's achievements in December 2008, when she was inducted into the California Hall of Fame, which is housed in the California Museum (formerly known as the California Museum for History, Women and the Arts) in

Sacramento. She certainly meets the criteria of individuals who embody "California's innovative spirit and have made their mark on history."

In 2014, Julia was also posthumously awarded the 2014 Gold Medal at the American Institute of Architects (AIA) Convention in Chicago, Illinois. She was nominated by female Chicago architect Jeanne Gang, who stated this in her nomination to the AIA board: "Julia Morgan was a true superstar. Julia received many glamorous commissions, but she continued to devote a large part of her talent to empowering the poor and vulnerable. This and many of the other themes in her work and practice make her a powerfully relevant model for contemporary architects."

Julia's grandniece, Ellen North, and her daughter, Lauren Woodland, accepted the award. Julia was the first woman to ever receive the highest honor in her profession.

But Julia will not be remembered through awards. Julia recognized this when she said, "My buildings will be my legacy . . . they will speak for me long after I'm gone." We are fortunate that we can still visit and admire a number of the buildings she designed that are still standing and being used throughout California. People who are lucky enough to buy a Julia Morgan house are not just purchasing a home; they are also buying a piece of art.

8

Tarea Hall Pittman
(1903–1991)

HITTING THE RADIO AIRWAVES
FOR CIVIL RIGHTS

On December 7, 1941, life changed dramatically in the United States. The surprise attack by Japan on Pearl Harbor in Hawaii on this date brought the country into World War II. Men were needed as soldiers, and when many rushed to join the military, numerous vacancies were left in war defense factories. Many of these factories, especially those building ships, were on the West Coast in the San Francisco Bay Area. Women were called upon to step in and work. One advertisement asked women, "Can you use an electric mixer? If so, you can learn to operate a drill." Rosie the Riveter became symbolic of the national effort to recruit females to step out of their roles as housewives and become workers for war industries. Since Rosie was pictured by the well-known artist Norman Rockwell and others as a riveter on aircraft, "Winnie the Welder" was the name given to women who worked at the many shipyards during the war.

Being a woman, Tarea Hall Pittman was happy to see women gain some status in industry. However, as an African American,

Portrait of Tarea Hall Pittman. –BANC PIC 1978.147:129,
Courtesy of the Bancroft Library, University of California, Berkeley

she was enraged by the discrimination and prejudice that black men and women were experiencing as they tried to get jobs. Even before the United States officially entered World War II, President Franklin D. Roosevelt had tried to rally US citizens to join the war effort. His radio broadcast on December 29, 1940, was a call for the nation to become a "great arsenal of democracy" in order to arm and support the Allies in Europe. Upset that war industries would not hire African American workers, the National Association for the Advancement of Colored People (NAACP), in conjunction with the National Urban League, warned Roosevelt that they would get one hundred thousand people to march on Washington and assemble on the White House lawn during the summer of 1941 if the president did not support equal opportunity. Consequently, Roosevelt issued Executive Order 8802 on June 25, 1941, which stated, "There shall be no discrimination in the employment of workers in defense industries and in government because of race, creed, color, or national origin."

So many people headed to California to find work that the World War II years have been called the "Second Gold Rush" in that state. Many African American men and women traveled to California from the southwestern and central states (especially Louisiana, Texas, Arkansas, and Oklahoma) to find work. Between 1940 and 1945, it is estimated that the black population of the Bay Area grew by 227 percent.

But legislation does not immediately change attitudes and practices. Discrimination was still rampant in the latter part of 1941 and 1942. Tarea organized protests against the shipyards owned by Henry J. Kaiser. The four Kaiser yards in Richmond, northeast of the city of San Francisco across the bay, constituted the largest shipbuilding operation on the Pacific Coast; they contributed greatly to the war effort by building 727 cargo ships.

But even when they were hired to assist with this work, African American men and women usually were given the most unskilled tasks that involved physical labor, such as cleaning up production debris. If they could prove their qualifications for a skilled position, lack of union membership could still be used against them, and leadership roles were off-limits. There was even resentment between African Americans who lived in California before the war and those who moved there. Black women had the roughest time. Only 10 percent of the women hired were African American.

Nevertheless, increased sensitivity to race can be observed in photos taken at that time. On May 7, 1943, black actress and singer Lena Horne launched the *SS George Washington Carver* at Richmond Shipyard No. 1 of the Kaiser Company. This was the second Liberty (cargo) ship to be named for an outstanding African American. The first was the *SS Booker T. Washington*, launched in 1942 by famed African American opera star Marian Anderson. Dorothea Lange and Ansel Adams, two renowned photographers of the day, created a photo essay for *Fortune* magazine on the war shipyards in Richmond, and African Americans are included in these photos, so it is evident that Tarea's efforts did help to change attitudes. But this was nothing new for Tarea; she had already been facing and fighting prejudice for years.

———•••———

Born in Bakersfield, California, on January 30, 1903, Tarea Susie Hall was the second child of William and Susie Pinkney Hall. She went by the nickname Ty. Both of her parents' families had been early African American settlers in Kern County. According to the 1890 US census, there were only 11,322 African Americans in the entire state at that time. Her mother's family came from South Carolina in 1882, so they would have been included in that count; her father's family did not move to California from Alabama until 1895. In the 1910 US census, her father reported that he was employed as an engineer in the brewery industry, although later he was identified as a farmer. Tarea had one brother, Marcus (born 1905), and four sisters, Eugenia (1901), Clarice (1906), Faricita (1912), and June (1914).

Although African Americans did not face as much prejudice as Native Americans, Chinese immigrants, and those of Mexican ancestry in California, they still were limited by the bounds of discrimination. They knew that some California cities were "sundown towns," where African Americans and other nonwhites were advised (often by a sign at the town line) to be gone when it got dark or face the consequences, such as being physically beaten. Things were somewhat better in Bakersfield, the largest city in Kern County, where Tarea lived. African Americans could not get jobs as store clerks or secretaries, but women worked as domestics and men were hired by the Santa Fe and Southern Pacific Railroads. Unlike the situation in many other towns, the black population residing there was not segregated into one area. Although Tarea did face some racial prejudice, her problems arose mainly outside the educational setting because she attended an integrated public school (Kern County Union High School). The California legislature had revised the state school law in 1880 so that separate schools for different racial groups were not allowed. In reality, the state did permit educational segregation of Native American and Asian American children until 1947.

With the African American population steadily increasing in California (it nearly doubled every ten years from 1910 until 1940), organized efforts to gain societal equality also expanded. The Los Angeles branch of the National Association for the Advancement of Colored People (NAACP) was formed in 1914. As Tarea's family was successful (her father and each of his brothers had his own farm) and active in community affairs, the Hall men were instrumental in establishing the Bakersfield branch of the NAACP.

After graduating from high school, Tarea attended Bakersfield Junior College (now Bakersfield College). She was the first black student to graduate from that school. In 1923, Tarea moved to Berkeley to continue her education at the University of California. Although she had visited the Los Angeles campus, she opted to head north because she knew some other Kern County students at Berkeley. Black students were not allowed to live in campus housing, so Tarea used family connections to find a place to stay. In 1925, her father bought a house in Berkeley, where Tarea lived with her mother, who moved there because of health problems, and her two younger sisters, Faricita and June. As a student in 1926, she attended the biennial conference of the National Association of Colored Women in Oakland. The keynote speaker was Mary McLeod Bethune, a well-known educator and civil rights activist. Tarea felt that Bethune "absolutely electrified people." She surely had an effect on Tarea's thinking about life.

In her early days on campus, Tarea had met a young dental student, William R. Pittman, at a social gathering. William was born in Birmingham, Alabama, and moved to California as a boy to live with an aunt and uncle. He took classes during the day and worked at the post office at night. The two married in 1927, and Tarea took time off from her education while her husband finished his degree in dentistry at Meharry Medical College in Nashville, Tennessee, in 1930. He had to transfer to Nashville because the administrators at the University of California's College of Dentistry in San Francisco told him they would not graduate an African American student. It was hard for William to make a living as a dentist during the Great Depression years (1929–1939), so he worked as a chauffeur for $80 a month and Tarea worked in a cannery. Money was so tight that at one point they had to borrow $500 to pay the taxes on their house.

Tarea did return to school but opted to change her major. Originally planning to teach, she did her student teaching at Prescott School in West Oakland. From this experience, she decided she wanted to work with children and families in a community setting rather than in a school. Tarea had to transfer to San Francisco State College (now San Francisco State University) for this program. She earned her BA in social service in 1939 and went on to earn an MA in social welfare from the University of California, Berkeley. Her thesis focused on the California Residence Law. People had to live in California for three years in order to be considered a resident. Tarea argued that this was a problem for people moving to California from some states because they lost their residency rights in their home states after one year of absence. Consequently, these people ended up in limbo—not eligible for any public welfare services in either state. Using data she collected as part of her educational program field placement at the Richmond Travelers Aid Society, she completed her thesis: "Operation of State and County Residence Requirements under the California Indigent Aid Law in Contra Costa County." Her work earned her a master's degree in 1946.

Tarea and her husband, who was the first African American dentist in Berkeley, lived at 2930 Grove Street (now Martin Luther King Jr. Way). William established his dental practice in their home. It also became a gathering place for black college students, and Tarea loved debating social issues with them. She also worked to integrate facilities on the Berkeley college campus, particularly the barbershop. Tarea became active in civic organizations such as the Alameda County Branch of the NAACP and served as president of the California State Association of Colored Women's Clubs from 1936 to 1938. Her duties included persuading black women to register and vote and finding funding for projects to help African American children. The Fannie Wall Children's Home (orphanage) and Day Nursery in Oakland was supported by her efforts.

In 1936, Tarea organized the West Coast branches of the National Negro Congress. The entire organization convened in Chicago February 14–16, 1936, for its first national convention. Tarea attended and served as one of the two California delegates on the General Resolutions Committee. The local chapter of the National Negro Congress wanted a way to publicize positive news about the African American community in the Bay Area, so it purchased time on a local radio station for a weekly news program. The resulting show, *Negroes in the News*, aired on Oakland radio station KLS, Warner Brothers,

Oakland (later changed to KWBR and later KDIA). The African American community in Berkeley and the Bay Area eagerly awaited this fifteen-minute broadcast on Sunday mornings. It spotlighted activities by the NAACP, the Urban League, churches, schools, and other Bay Area African American groups and also shared the accomplishments of African Americans nationwide. Listeners could call in with comments or questions. As the host, Tarea shared news in what was described as a "regal-sounding voice." Her stories came from local and national sources such as the Associated Negro Press and black newspapers such as the *Los Angeles Sentinel* (still in existence) and *California Eagle*. After a brief period of time, the National Negro Congress decided to stop funding the show. Tarea, C. L. Dellums (president of the Brotherhood of Sleeping Car Porters, the first international black labor union to achieve standing in the American Federation of Labor), and some colleagues then formed the Negro Educational Council of the East Bay and recruited sponsors to cover the cost of the airtime. Tarea hosted the show for over forty years, becoming a nationally recognized radio personality. She also worked as a social worker in San Francisco and Contra Costa County during part of this time.

When the United States entered World War II, many blacks headed to the West Coast to find employment. It is estimated that more than forty-six thousand African Americans moved to the Bay Area between 1941 and 1945. Tarea not only helped those new arrivals integrate into the local communities, especially Oakland and Richmond, she also organized the protests against the discrimination occurring in the local war industries.

After the war, Tarea continued her civil rights work. She served as president of the California Council of Negro Women from 1948 to 1951, working to provide more child care centers, preschool education, and health care for black children. She pushed to desegregate the Oakland Fire Department in 1952. That same year, she started working for the NAACP as field secretary. In 1956, her efforts helped the NAACP get the book *Little Black Sambo* banned from public school libraries in Alameda County, citing its reinforcement of negative stereotypes of African Americans. Tarea also served as the legislative advocate who followed and tried to influence legislation for the Fair Employment Practices Committee, a group comprised of various organizations, including the NAACP. Her lobbying efforts for that group helped produce the California Fair Employment Practices bill, which was signed into law in 1959 by Governor Edmund Brown. It prohibited businesses as well as labor unions from discriminating against employees or people seeking employment based on race, color, national origin, ancestry, or religious beliefs. Tarea was named acting regional director of the NAACP in 1959, and two years later she became regional director.

Under Tarea's direction, the fight for fair housing by the NAACP continued. In 1960, she testified before the US Commission on Civil Rights, asserting that "residential segregation based on race is the general rule in the towns and cities in the West." She also noted in her annual NAACP summary for that year that "hard core resistance to integrated housing" was the most prevalent problem for African Americans in the West. The California Fair Housing Act (better known as the Rumford Act for its sponsor, Assemblyman William Byron Rumford) was passed in 1963 by the legislature. The act decreed that property owners could not deny people housing because of race, religion, sex, or national origin. However, it was not totally successful. As Tarea stated, "To talk about the fact that we're making headway, is just to bury your head in the sand. In my lifetime, I have seen segregation and discrimination spread across California. It's a creeping paralysis."

In 1964, discrimination efforts in housing became more open. Proposition 14, which appeared on the ballot that year, was an initiative attempting to give landlords and property owners the right to decline to sell or rent residential properties as they chose. The NAACP participated in a coalition called Californians Against Proposition 14, which organized a voter registration drive and challenged the constitutionality of the proposition in the courts.

Martin Luther King Jr. assisted their efforts and stated at a rally in Los Angeles that "men hate each other because they fear, they fear because they do not know one another, and they do not know one another because they are separated."

Although the initiative was passed by California voters, it was later ruled unconstitutional by the California Supreme Court, a ruling upheld by the US Supreme Court in 1967.

Tarea served as NAACP regional director until 1965, when she became director of the NAACP Special Contribution Fund for the West Coast Region, remaining in that role until 1970. She also continued to broadcast the *Negroes in the News* radio program into the late 1970s. In 1971 she became the fundraiser for the western region of the Opportunity Industrial Centers. Their purpose today, as it was then, is "fighting for economic and racial justice through workforce development of underserved and underrepresented communities." After an extended illness, she passed away on July 31, 1991, in San Francisco at eighty-eight years of age. Her husband, William, who practiced dentistry for over forty-four years before retiring in June 1975, had died in 1984.

In 2015, a community effort was begun to rename the South Branch Library in Berkeley for Tarea Hall Pittman. The library is close to the location where the Pittmans lived. One supporter of the name change was retired journalist and former professional baseball player Charles Aikens. He recalled that one Sunday morning he heard Tarea mention his name on her radio show. From 1962 to 1964 he played with the Baltimore Orioles, and he felt honored to hear her speak about his baseball career. According to Aikens, her radio program "helped people to feel pride in themselves after it had been taken away from them for over two hundred years of slavery." After considering the widespread community support, the Berkeley Board of Library Trustees voted to recommend to the city council that the South Branch Library be renamed for Tarea Hall Pittman. The city council accepted the recommendation in June 2015, and the facility is now the Tarea Hall Pittman South Branch Library.

Although Tarea Hall Pittman's actual occupation for many years was social worker, she also spent much of her personal time working for civil rights in her community. C L. Dellums once called her "the best-known Negro woman in California," but she gained recognition outside California because of her NAACP duties and her radio program. Her efforts to garner equality of opportunity became her life's work. She delivered hundreds of speeches about social conditions up and down the West Coast, and people listened to her because she was articulate and well informed. She hoped to empower others by sharing what she knew either in person or via the airwaves. We probably will never really know all she did, as she tells us:

> It would never be possible for us to really get a full overview of the work, the struggle, the amount of labor that it took and the fidelity that people had to really exhibit, to follow through. . . . I think that it is a very good thing that we are documenting what was being done because already—take a person like me who was working directly in it—there are so many things . . . pivotal things that we now have lost sight of and they have just been lost. I was an official of the NAACP; we had no research department. Our primary officers that were coordinating the lay activities were so busy that many of the documentary vehicles that we had have simply been lost. We were so busy doing that we didn't record a number of things that in retrospect I can see were very important.

But what remains does verify that Tarea was a key figure in the civil rights and social-welfare-equalization efforts in the area around San Francisco and along the entire West Coast for a large portion of the twentieth century. She recognized problems and tried to find solutions. Her tireless pursuit to better the lives of African Americans resulted in significant societal changes during her lifetime and ultimately led to improvements in lifestyle for Californians of many backgrounds in future years.

9

Yoshiko Uchida

(1921–1992)

FROM INTERNMENT TO JAPANESE
AMERICAN PIONEER OF CHILDREN'S LITERATURE

It was Sunday afternoon, December 7, 1941, and the Uchida family was ready to enjoy lunch. Yoshiko planned to eat quickly because she needed to go to the library at the University of California, Berkeley, where she was a senior. Exams started in a few days and she had to study. Suddenly, a voice broke into the programs on the radio announcing that the Japanese had attacked Pearl Harbor in Hawaii. The family believed someone was just playing a prank, so Yoshiko went to the campus and studied the entire afternoon.

The minute she returned home, Yoshiko knew something was very wrong. Her father wasn't in the house and a strange man sat in the living room. Her mother explained that two agents from the Federal Bureau of Investigation (FBI) had taken her father away for questioning. One agent stayed behind to guard the remaining family and prevent them from communicating with anyone else by phone or in person.

Although the guard finally left that night, her father did not return. Five days later, the family learned that he was being held at the immigration detention center in San Francisco, and Mr. Uchida was not the only one. All of the leaders of the Japanese American community in the San Francisco Bay Area were being detained. The Uchida family arranged for permission to visit Yoshiko's father and learned he was being sent to a prisoner-of-war camp in Missoula, Montana, because he was *Issei* (first-generation Japanese immigrant). US law at the time prohibited Issei Japanese immigrants from becoming US citizens. When the United States declared war on Japan on December 8 of that year, Mr. Uchida had become an "enemy alien."

Yoshiko's older sister, who had been born in the United States and thus was a US citizen, took over the family affairs. But each

Yoshiko Uchida autographing her books for young fans in 1984. —The Yoshiko Uchida photograph collection, BANC PIC 1986.059:273, courtesy of the Bancroft Library, University of California, Berkeley

day brought challenges. Their finances had been blocked so they only had a little money. Important papers in their safety deposit box could not be accessed because the FBI took all of the keys. The Uchida family had done nothing wrong, but because they looked like the enemy, they became the target for harassment in many ways.

On February 19, 1942, President Franklin D. Roosevelt signed Executive Order 9066. It authorized the establishment of military zones from which Japanese Americans, German Americans, and Italian Americans could be removed. Consequently, the US Secretary of War ordered that Japanese Americans, regardless of US citizenship or length of residence in the country, be removed from the West Coast of the United States as a military necessity and held in internment camps. Although this order violated the Fifth Amendment (guarantee of due process of law) and Fourteenth Amendment (equal protection under the law for all citizens) of the US Constitution, the US Supreme Court supported the decision. While the United States was also at war with Germany and Italy, it was primarily Japanese Americans who were targeted by the edict; German Americans and Italian Americans were largely unaffected. The order did not include Hawaii, which was closer to Japan and where more than a third of the population was Japanese American.

Although the Uchidas had experienced prejudice before while living in California, this seemed like a direct attack on them and others of Japanese heritage. Yoshiko was stunned and hurt when a close Caucasian friend asked her if she had known about the attack on Pearl Harbor before it happened. She was an American, not a traitor.

The Uchida's evacuation order came through on April 21. Each family was given a number. The Uchidas became 13453. On May 1, they were to be sent to Tanforan Racetrack, a horse-racing facility in San Bruno, California, that had quickly been converted into an "assembly center." The family had to clear their belongings out of the house they had lived in for fifteen years because the government rule was people could only take with them what they could carry. The hardest decision for the Uchidas was what to do with their dog, Laddie. Finally, Yoshiko thought to put an ad in the *Daily Californian* newspaper at the university: "I am one of the Japanese American students soon to be evacuated and have a male Scotch Collie that can't come with me. Can anyone please give him a home? If interested, please call me immediately at Berkeley 7646W."

The day the ad appeared, Yoshiko had numerous phone calls offering to take the dog. She gave him to the first boy who called, as he seemed to be someone who would take good care of their pet. Now if her family could also be given the same amount of concern and kindness, perhaps the future would not seem so bleak.

———•••———

Life had seemed so bright for Yoshiko before December 7. Her father, Takashi "Dwight" Uchida had come to California in 1906 right after the great earthquake in San Francisco. He had dreams of attending Yale University in New Haven, Connecticut, to become a doctor. However, he ended up in store management with various Japanese companies. In 1917, he went to work for Mitsui & Company, an international trading firm in San Francisco. That same year, he married Iku Umegaki, with whom he had corresponded for a year. They had never met before but were brought together by professors at Doshisha University in Kyoto, which they both attended. Because Dwight had a salaried position as an assistant manager, his and Iku's lives were somewhat better than other immigrants.

Keiko was born March 15, 1918, almost four years before Yoshiko, who was born November 24, 1921, in Alameda. The Uchida family lived in a cheerful, three-bedroom house in Berkeley. A huge backyard hosted a sandbox, swings, and hammock as well as various fruit trees and berry bushes. Although Yoshiko did not attend Japanese language school, as did many *Nisei* (second-generation Japanese immigrants), her house was filled with paintings, pottery, and other Japanese artwork. Using the pen name Yukari, her mother often wrote *tanka* poems, a classic Japanese poetry form using thirty-one syllables. The family always remembered its roots as Yoshiko later wrote, "It was as though a long invisible thread would always bind Mama and Papa to the country they had left behind. And that thread seemed to wind just as surely around Keiko and me as well."

Yoshiko often felt the duality of her position in society. She once described her early life as "hot dogs and bamboo shoots." This was especially evident when she attended an event at the 1932 Summer Olympic Games in Los Angeles. She was dressed in a red, white, and blue outfit and cheered for the American team. Her cousins, who lived in the Japanese American community in that city and took lessons in the Japanese language, rooted for the Japanese athletes. Yoshiko felt she was truly an American. She used the name Yoshi and her sister used the name Kay to help them fit in.

Yoshiko showed an early interest in writing. At the age of ten, she wrote stories such as "Jimmy Chipmunk and His Friends—A Short Story for Small Children" and "Willie, the Squirrel" on brown wrapping paper. Two years later, she used her father's typewriter to compose a seven-chapter book titled "Sally Jane Waters." She attended Longfellow School in Berkeley (which still exists today as a middle school) and University High School in Oakland, which she completed in just two-and-a-half years. She was sixteen when she entered the University of California, Berkeley.

Therefore, being forced in 1942 to leave all she knew was devastating. Arriving at Tanforan Assembly Center with her mother and sister, and seeing the high barbed-wire fence and guard towers with armed soldiers, Yoshiko felt humiliated and hurt. Why was the US government treating her this way when she was an American? The family was assigned quarters in Barracks 16, which turned out to be a horse stable, and apartment 40 was one of the stalls. This ten-by-twenty-foot space was their new home. Yoshiko later described her living conditions: "Dust, dirt, and wood shavings covered the linoleum that had been laid over manure-covered boards, the smell of horses hung in the air, and the whitened corpses of many insects still clung to the hastily white-washed walls."

There was no privacy, with a stall behind theirs as well as on either side. The walls of the stalls were so thin that every word that was spoken could be heard by others. Sometimes people brazenly knocked on the wall and asked that a remark be repeated when they didn't catch it. There were no doors in the latrines. This especially bothered the older women, who covered their faces with newspapers or dragged large cardboard boxes to use as screens. Nothing in the camp was finished. Meals were mainly beans and bread. Yoshiko's mother wrote:

Plate in hand,

I stand in line,

Losing my resolve

To hide my tears.

—Yukari

One bright spot in their days at Tanforan was that Dwight was able to join them. Another was that Yoshiko was awarded her bachelor of arts degree in English, philosophy, and history that she earned at the University of California, Berkeley. She couldn't attend the commencement because of her internment, but she received her diploma rolled in a cardboard container in the mail. She graduated with cum laude honors. The family stayed at the Tanforan Assembly Center for five months before being transferred to the Central Utah Relocation Center—better known as Topaz—near Delta, Utah.

Located in the Sevier Desert, Topaz was nothing like its public relations name—Jewel of the Desert. Tar-papered barracks had been hastily built on barren, powdery sand, again surrounded with barbed wire and guard towers, which the internees were told was for their protection. The instruction sheet they received upon arrival said the following: "You are now in Topaz, Utah. Here we say Dining Hall and not Mess Hall; Safety Council, not Internal Police; Residents, not Evacuees; and last but not least, Mental Climate, not Morale."

Words did not help make their situation better. Almost eight thousand people were sent to this camp, which was only about one square mile in size. That made it, at the time, the fifth-largest city in the state of Utah. The temperature at night often dropped well below freezing, while daytime temperatures soared to ninety degrees. Dust storms made it hard to breathe and blanketed their possessions with sand. Yoshiko's mother wrote:

> The fury of the
>
> Dust storm spent,
>
> I gaze through tears
>
> At the sunset glow.
>
> —Yukari

The supply of water into the camp went on and off sporadically. The camp was in such a state of disorganization that the evacuees soon formed their own committees to solve problems. Both Keiko and Yoshiko applied to work in the two elementary schools that were created. Yoshiko taught second grade. Snakes and scorpions sometimes shared the room with her students. She later described this period of her life:

> I worked hard to be a good teacher; I went to meetings, wrote long letters to my friends, knitted sweaters and socks, devoured any books I could find, listened to the radio, went to art school and to church and to lectures by outside visitors. . . . I also had a wisdom tooth removed at the hospital and suffered a swollen face for three days. I caught one cold after another; I fell on the unpaved roads; I lost my voice from the dust; I got homesick and angry and despondent. And sometimes I cried.

The War Relocation Authority (WRA) did allow individuals to leave the internment camps under certain conditions. These included (1) the person had a place to go and could find a means of self-support; (2) FBI and other intelligence records indicated the individual was not a threat to national security; (3) there was no evidence that the person's presence in the selected community would cause problems for the public; and (4) the WRA would be informed of the person's whereabouts at all times. Yoshiko and her sister both applied to leave Topaz and were released May 24, 1943. Yoshiko left for a graduate fellowship in education at Smith College in Northampton, Massachusetts. Her sister left the same day to assume a position at a nursery school run by Mount Holyoke College in South Hadley, Massachusetts. Yoshiko noted, "I left Topaz determined to work hard and prove that I was as loyal as any other American." Her mother celebrated their release:

> The budding plum
>
> Holds my own joy
>
> At the melting ice
>
> And the long winter's end.
>
> —Yukari

Yoshiko used her full scholarship wisely. She earned a master's in education in 1944.

Like her mother, Yoshiko grappled with her negative wartime experiences through writing. After teaching first and second grades for several years at Frankford Friends School, a Quaker school outside of Philadelphia, Pennsylvania, Yoshiko decided to quit teaching and find a line of work that would provide her with more writing time. She moved to New York City and worked as a secretary during the day and wrote stories at night. Her focus was writing for adults until her children's book *The Dancing Kettle and Other Japanese Folk Tales* was published in 1949. After this great success, she concentrated her efforts more on writing picture books

Yoshiko and her sister Keiko preparing to leave Topaz. From left: Yoshiko, mother Iku, father Dwight, and Keiko. –The Yoshiko Uchida photograph collection, BANC PIC 1986.059:215, courtesy of the Bancroft Library, University of California, Berkeley

and books for school-age children. She explained, "I wanted to write stories about human beings, not the stereotypic Asian. There weren't any books like that in the early '50s when I started writing for children."

In 1952, she was awarded a Ford Foundation fellowship in Japan, where she studied Japanese culture, customs, and folktales. Spending two years there (one year in Kyoto and the other in Tokyo) helped Yoshiko learn and have a better appreciation for her own ancestry.

Returning to the United States, she lived in Oakland, California, and cared for her parents, who were both in poor health. She continued writing but stayed with collections of Japanese folktales because she didn't think Americans were ready for true stories of Japanese Americans during the war. Yoshiko explained, "There was still a lot of hostility about the war. I wasn't sure a publisher would accept it." After the publication of her tenth book, she quit a day job as a secretary and focused all of her time on writing. She wrote the first drafts of her books in pen on the backs of junk mail, stating, "I have inherited frugal Issei habits." These drafts were later typed on a typewriter for submission to publishers.

Yoshiko's mother died in 1966 and her father lived until 1971. Feeling now that the time was right, Yoshiko then moved into her own apartment in Berkeley. She spent the remainder of her life writing and speaking about her wartime experiences, especially to children. *Journey to Topaz* (1971) was a fictional account of her time in Utah, and *Journey Home* (1978) was a fictional account of her family's postcamp days. It took her years to tell her real story for young adult readers in her autobiography, *Desert Exile: The Uprooting of a Japanese American Family* (1982). Yoshiko created a body of Japanese American literature for children where none had previously existed. She wanted children to understand the true events of the past: "When I asked a group of fifth graders to tell me who was president of the United States during World War II, I was surprised by the long silence that followed. Finally, a very small voice ventured a guess, 'George Washington?'"

Over the course of her writing career, Yoshiko published almost forty books, including nonfiction for adults and fiction for children and teenagers. While her personal accounts relate to the World War II era, she also wrote from the Japanese American perspective about other historical events, including the Wakamatsu Tea and Silk Farm Colony Experiment in California in 1869 (*Samurai of Gold Hill*, 1972) and the Great Depression (*A Jar of Dreams*, 1993).

Yoshiko's books have won awards and recognition from many professional organizations, including the American Library

Association, the International Reading (now Literacy) Association, the National Council for the Social Studies, and the National Council of Teachers of English. In 1988, the Japanese American Citizens League honored her with the Japanese American of the Biennium award for outstanding achievement.

Many years after the internment of the Japanese Americans, the US government reviewed its actions. In 1976, President Gerald R. Ford revoked Executive Order 9066, remarking, "Not only was that evacuation wrong, but Japanese-Americans were and are loyal Americans." President Jimmy Carter continued this sentiment. The Commission on Wartime Relocation and Internment of Civilians (CWRIC) was created during his presidency in 1980. Public hearings were held across the nation and over 750 people testified. In 1983, the CWRIC issued its findings in a report titled *Personal Justice Denied*. It stated that the incarceration of Japanese Americans had not been justified by military necessity. Rather, the decision to confine Japanese American people was due to "race prejudice, war hysteria, and a failure of political leadership."

In 1988, the US Congress passed the Civil Liberties Act, which President Ronald Reagan signed on August 10 of that year. This bill was intended to repay some of the financial losses of the Japanese Americans uprooted during World War II. However, it did not go into effect until October 1990, when nine elderly Japanese men each received a check for $20,000 and a letter of formal apology signed by President George H. W. Bush. Other surviving internees or their heirs were compensated through 1993.

For many Issei (and some Nisei), this admission of wrong and attempt at compensation came too late. Yoshiko was one of the lucky ones who was still alive. She addressed why she thought she had survived internment in her 1982 autobiography: "Perhaps I survived the uprooting and incarceration because my Issei parents taught me to endure. Perhaps I survived because at the time I believed I was taking the only viable path and believed what I was doing was right. Looking back now, I think the survival of the Japanese through those tragic, heartbreaking days was a triumph of the human spirit."

Yoshiko was a small woman (she stood barely five feet tall), and poor health eventually took its toll. After fighting chronic fatigue syndrome for several years, Yoshiko died of a stroke on June 21, 1992, at age seventy in Berkeley. In her words, her legacy was "to stress the positive aspects of life that I want children to value and cherish. I hope they can be caring human beings who don't think in terms of labels—foreigners or Asians or whatever—but think of people as human beings. If that comes across, then I've accomplished my purpose."

Fans from all over the United States had written letters to Yoshiko over the years. One child noted that reading *Journey to Topaz* gave her "a sharp pain in my heart." The huge amount of correspondence that is part of the Yoshiko Uchida collection in the Bancroft Library at the University of California, Berkeley, is a testament that this child and other readers of Yoshiko's books got her message.

Rose Ann Vuich in the California State Senate after her 1976 election. –Associated Press photo

10

Rose Ann Vuich

(1927–2001)

CHANGING THE CALIFORNIA STATE SENATE WITH A BELL

The bell rang loudly in the California State Senate chamber. The groans of the men followed. Some glanced toward a certain seat. Not again! They knew the sound was a reminder from Rose Ann Vuich, the first female member of the California State Senate, that somebody had forgotten and addressed the assembly as "gentlemen of the senate" or "fellow senators." To make sure the other state senators remembered that there was a woman present, she kept a small bell (opinion varies about whether it was brass or porcelain) on her desk and shook it vigorously whenever one of her colleagues used gender-biased language. She was going to "break them of that habit." When Rose was elected a California senator in 1976, there was not a bathroom in the capitol (the building where a state legislature meets) for women legislators—only for men. The state had to convert a closet into a bathroom for her. This rose-colored room is still called the Rose Room in her honor.

After Rose began her term in the upper house of the legislature in 1977, the phrase "What's in it for Dinuba?"—the farm town southeast of Fresno where she lived—was also often heard. Her colleagues quickly learned that she studied every detail of their proposed bills, questioning the figures, the rationale for passage, and most important to her, what good, if any, her "yes" vote on a bill might bring to the people who had elected her. Although the other senators might have resented at times what they called her "nitpicking," she also gained bipartisan respect for her unshakable honesty and refusal to make deals on so-called juice bills. These were bills that provided little benefit to the state but brought campaign contributions to the lawmakers who proposed and supported them. Although a Democrat, Rose did not always follow the party line. She consistently reflected the conservative and agricultural views of her district. She would often bring fresh produce such as apricots, plums, and nectarines to the state senate to share. Before her hungry peers could enjoy the fruit, however, Rose would explain how the agricultural industry was important to the overall health of the entire state. She was a forceful advocate for that cause as well as a role model and a positive leader for women. In presentations to children, she would state, "When someone tells you a woman can't do that, just remember the name of California's first woman state senator." She served in the state senate for sixteen years. That was quite an accomplishment for a farm girl from the Central Valley who worked hard to get the otherwise all-male state senate to stop calling her "our little lady."

———•••———

Rose Ann Vuich was a second-generation Serbian American. Known as Rosie to family and friends (and listed as Rosie O. in the 1930 US census), she was born in January 1927 in Cutler, California. Official federal and state records vary as to what day, but the California Birth Index lists it as the 29th. Rose grew up on her parents' farm near Cutler in Tulare County. Her father, Obren J. Vuich, and mother, Stana Stella Runjavac Vuich, were Yugoslav immigrants, so their native language was not English. They had immigrated to the United States in 1899. Rose had an older brother, William Obren Vuich (1924–1997). The farm was successful and included a small packinghouse next to the house to wrap and ship the family's crops. A white peach the family grew and marketed was called the "Rose Ann" in honor of their daughter.

After graduating from Orosi Union High School (now Orosi High School), Rose attended Central California Commercial College in Fresno and graduated with a degree in accounting. She opened her own business in nearby Dinuba (also Tulare County), which became her home for the rest of her life. Although her days were filled as a tax consultant, estate planner, and helping to manage the family's farm, she felt it was important also to be involved in local community activities. Rose joined the board of the Alta Hospital District and was a member of the agricultural review committee for the Tulare County Fair. After her father died in 1940, her mother and brother had to work even harder to keep the farm prosperous. They were so successful that they eventually acquired three other ranches. Although Rose helped with the family business (180 acres of citrus, olive, and fruit trees) when she could, its success allowed her to pursue other activities. She was the first woman from Tulare County to be elected president of the Dinuba Chamber of Commerce in the 1950s.

Although she had been active in Democratic Party politics in Tulare County for twelve years, serving on the county central committee, Rose did not seek a political career. Fate stepped in to change that in 1976. The Democratic candidate everyone assumed would run withdrew from the state senate race, and Rose was chosen to replace him. Many people believed that her Republican opponent, Ernest Mobley, was a shoo-in for the position. Even her own party felt she had little chance. They applauded Rose's willingness to run but did not feel she could compete with her opponent's political connections. He was a ten-year veteran assemblyman and a savvy campaigner. Consequently, they gave Rose little financial support for her political efforts. But that didn't deter Rose. She stated that she "tore into that campaign and campaigned from morning till night, in my own grassroots, down-to-earth way." She found that she had enough funds for one thirty-second television ad. What should she say? She decided to follow a strategy that she would adhere to throughout her political career: let her constituents know that she was looking out for their interests. The ad denounced her opponent for supporting the funding of a southern California freeway while failing to seek money for State Highway 41 in their own district. Voters agreed with Rose, and the "Freeway Lady," as they began calling her, was elected. It was one of the biggest political upsets in the state. Of the four women running in state senate races that year, Rose was the only one to win.

When a news reporter remarked that she would attract a lot of publicity when she took her place in the state senate in January, she was pleased. "That's great. I'll be a better asset to my district if I get more attention from the press. It will be a help to our agricultural area." When the day arrived, however, Rose was emotional: "I drove up in front of the Capitol building, and I just sat there a long time, looking up at the dome. And then I took a deep breath and said to myself, 'Well, old girl, here you are. Give it all you've got, because that's what you promised the people back home.'"

At the swearing-in ceremony, Rose noted later that her eyes filled with tears. "I had to tell myself, now don't start bawling or they'll say, 'Typical woman.'" Rose took to her new position quickly and started asking tough questions about legislation being considered by the state senate. Her accounting background was very useful in spotting financial errors in bills. Always an advocate for her beloved Central Valley agriculture (her district included Fresno and Tulare Counties), Rose created California's Agricultural Export Finance Program (SB 1196, Chapter 1693, Statutes of 1984). It provided technical and monetary resources, especially to small and medium-sized businesses, to increase the export of goods, services, and agricultural products produced in California. This legislation became a national model. It has been recognized by the Council of State Governments as one of most innovative state programs to help small businesses. Rose also wrote the legislation that created the California Trade and Commerce Agency (SB 1909, Chapter 1364, Statutes of 1992). That agency is credited with helping pull California out of recession in the early 1990s. The organization lasted in the state from 1992 until 2004.

As chair of the legislature's rural caucus, Rose traveled extensively throughout her district and the state. She attended and spoke at local functions as her schedule permitted. Besides her position in the state senate, she also participated in the US Secretary of Interior's task force that was studying a 1902 law that limited the use of US Bureau of Reclamation project water. Signed by President Theodore Roosevelt, this act authorized the sale of public land in 160-acre lots to pay for the construction of dams and canals to irrigate the West. People who bought this property had first rights to the water and paid lower fees. Speaking at the Terra Bella Chamber of Commerce in Tulare County in 1977, she stated, "Whatever changes are made in that law, it will affect every area in the United States that depends on a government water project." This was also a personal issue for her because of her family's farms: "We on the east side will be left high and dry if they divide those huge parcels on the west side into 160-acre plots and sell to 80,000 persons. The water level on the higher east side will be drawn down by the deep wells those 80,000 will have to dig on the west side to farm their 160 acres. It is not feasible. It can't be done. Even if the land were free, you couldn't make a living on that land."

In 1984, Rose authored two bills that directly affected agriculture. SB 1320 (Chapter 578, Statutes of 1984) set fines of up to $25,000 for any person who started or spread an infestation of a plant, pest, or animal. SB 1623 (Chapter 506, Statutes of 1984) allocated money to aid in the control and eradication of boll weevils, an insect that attacks cotton, which was an important crop in California.

Rose also worked tirelessly to get State Highway 41 in Fresno constructed. She successfully lobbied in 1978 to secure the funding necessary to complete this crosstown freeway that had been abandoned halfway through construction that began in 1970. Rose considered its completion her proudest accomplishment because that had been the key point of her 1976 election campaign.

In 1985, Rose was instrumental in the formation of the California Legislative Women's Caucus (a caucus is a group of people united to promote a cause). It included nine Democrats and six Republicans from both the state senate and the assembly. Formally recognized by the Joint Rules Committee, women proved that they had finally countered the comment that Rose had had to fight: "You're taking a seat of a man." According to the caucus's bylaws today, its purpose is to "encourage collegiality, participation in and cooperation among elected women in California government and to promote the interests of women, children and families through legislation." The original intent of the caucus was to fight sexism in the legislature, both subtle and overt. Since some male legislators sneered and laughed when the subject of the women's caucus was initially mentioned on the assembly floor that year, its necessity seems obvious.

That same year, 1985, Rose was inducted into the California Public Education Hall of Fame. This honor recognizes graduates of California public schools who have made significant contributions to society. The award was presented at the annual convention of the California School Boards Association held in San Francisco in December. In 1986, Rose also supported education by attending the name-change ceremony of her alma mater, Central California Commercial College, which became Heald College, Fresno Campus.

Rose eventually became chairman of the Senate Banking, Commerce, and International Trade Committee. Her upright character was solidified in the public's view during a federal trial in 1989–1990. The FBI had conducted a sting operation during the political corruption scandals involving several legislators in Sacramento in the mid to late 1980s. A phony special-interest bill had been floated by several legislators, and one accepted a bribe to support it. Rose was called as a prosecution witness in the trial of one senator, who was charged with extortion, racketeering, and money laundering. Part of the evidence presented in the trial was a tape-recording in which one of the senator's aides stated that the bogus bill shouldn't be sent to the Vuich-led banking committee because she "doesn't play ball." Although the senator tried to smear Rose during his trial by calling her "a sick old lady" who had difficulty remembering events of 1988, he was convicted and received monetary fines and a six-and-a-half-year sentence in federal prison.

In another example of Rose's unwavering dedication to what she thought was right, she was a key vote in 1986 against the construction of a prison in Los Angeles, citing high costs and asserting that there were less-expensive building sites available.

In 1977, Rose had won the praise of Republican George Deuk-mejian, then majority leader in the state senate, who called her "an independent individual [who] is not going to be dictated to either by the governor's office or by the leaders of the legislature. We have concluded that every decision she makes is in an honest and independent fashion."

But Deukmejian's tune changed in 1988 when he was governor of California and Rose was one of those who voted no on the confirmation of Dan Lungren for state treasurer. Governor Deukmejian had appointed fellow Republican Lungren as California's acting state treasurer and expected Rose to support Lungren's appointment because she had often told the people in her district "how helpful and supportive she is of the governor." Deukmejian also told reporters that he would think more favorably about the bills of lawmakers who supported Lungren. Although it was well known that Rose always did what she thought was best for her constituents, there was an audible gasp from members of both political parties when she voted "no." Lungren lost confirmation by one vote, an outcome that was later upheld by the state supreme court. Rose's action did not sit well with many politicians in the state, who labeled her persona non grata (Latin for an "unacceptable" or "unwelcome person"). They worked to defeat Rose's reelection. It didn't work. She defeated her challengers so badly in 1980 (garnering 72 percent of the vote) and 1984 (with 76 percent) that no one even ran against her in 1988. She was so popular in her district that it was once stated, "Anything she does is gold." It is believed that she probably could have run unopposed again and won, but she chose to retire from the state senate in 1992.

According to an interview given by her brother to the Associated Press in 1995, Rose was bedridden after she left the state senate. She died on August 30, 2001, in Dinuba, the cause of death recorded as complications of Parkinson's and Alzheimer's diseases. Her remains are in the Chapel of the Light Columbarium in Fresno, California. Beside her name, it proudly states on her burial vault that she was the first woman senator in California.

Rose Ann Vuich is remembered in many ways in California. Established in 1998, the Rose Ann Vuich Ethical Leadership Award is sponsored by the Fresno Business Council, the *Fresno Bee*, and the Kenneth L. Maddy Institute of Public Affairs at California State University, Fresno. It is awarded annually to an elected official who has demonstrated the qualities Rose exhibited in her political career: "integrity, strength of character, exemplary ethical behavior, ability to build consensus, serving the public interest and vision for enhancing the community." The 2004 winner was Calvin M. Dooley, who was Rose's administrative assistant from 1987 to 1990 and went on to serve in the US House of Representatives from 1991 to 2005. In his tribute to Rose before the US Congress on September 6, 2001, he stated, "I learned from Rose Ann the virtue and dedication of public service, and the importance of standing up for what is right."

In 1997, the interchange between State Highway 41 and State Highway 180 in the City of Fresno was named the Rose Ann Vuich Interchange (Senate Concurrent Resolution 25, Chapter 85), commemorating all her efforts to get those two highways constructed. At the California State Capitol, Hearing Room 2040 was renamed the Rose Ann Vuich Hearing Room in 2006. A large oil painting of her hangs in that room. In 2015, the room was rededicated and portraits of the forty-one women who became senators after Rose were added.

Rose is also remembered by the people she served in Tulare County. Rose Ann Vuich Park was created in her hometown of Dinuba. With her love of agriculture, Rose would be pleased that the Raisin Harvest Festival is held at that site each September. Also in Dinuba, the car Rose rode in when participating in parades is housed by the Alta District Historical Society (ADHS). Rose supported this local organization with a $50,000 donation in October 1991. There is also a display of photos, plaques, and other mementos about her in the ADHS White House Cultural Center. Rose was one of the ten women spotlighted in the 2015 Tulare County Library exhibit entitled "Women of Tulare County." The exhibit ran throughout March as a celebration of Women's History Month. Each year, the Tulare County Democratic Central Committee also sponsors the Rose Ann Vuich Dinner and Awards Presentation in her honor.

Rose did not consider herself a feminist. If anyone asked, her response was always that she was "not a part of the women's liberation movement." She never married, and she lived with her mother most of her life. Rose proved, however, that being a woman was not an obstruction to providing courageous leadership. Subsequent women legislators have her to thank for breaking up the all-male world of the California State Senate and making that male culture more open to the inclusion of women. Two years after Rose was elected in 1976 another woman joined her in the state senate: Diane Watson from Los Angeles. When Rose retired in 1992, there were five female senators.

Although Rose's surname has been anglicized, it is derived from the given name Vuja, a diminutive of the masculine name Vuk, which means "wolf" in Serbian. Through her intelligence, protectiveness of her pack (her constituents), and aggressiveness when needed, Rose demonstrated the characteristics of her namesake, qualities that made both of them powerful in their worlds. Rose's life as a hardworking, independent public servant should remain as a model of great leadership to both women and men in California and beyond.

11
Shirley Temple Black
(1928–2014)

A HOLLYWOOD AND POLITICAL STAR

Her bouncing blonde curls and angelic face always caught people's attention. By 1935, people from all over the world also knew her name: Shirley Temple. That included Franklin Delano Roosevelt (FDR) and his wife, Eleanor. With the Great Depression gripping the United States, the president and first lady knew that publicity of them interacting with the cheerful child star loved by the American people would be viewed positively. The president even stated, "As long as our country has Shirley Temple, we will be all right. When the spirit of the people is lower than at any other time during this Depression, it is a splendid thing that for just fifteen cents, an American can go to a movie and look at the smiling face of a baby and forget his troubles."

So, Shirley was invited to the White House on February 27, 1935. She remembered that she "liked the President a lot. I had lost a tooth just before I met him. Franklin said, 'I'm concerned! Shirley Temple is supposed to smile a lot.' Well, I wouldn't smile, because I was trying to cover up my lost tooth, because I was embarrassed by it." The photo shoot did not go well.

In 1936, Shirley created a pretend police force that included the "official" Shirley Temple Badge, which she gave away to special people she met. J. Edgar Hoover, director of the FBI, became a member of the Shirley Temple Police Force in 1937. Eleanor Roosevelt visited the Hollywood set where Shirley was making the movie *Little Miss Broadway* on March 18, 1938. Shirley gave her two badges to give to her grandchildren with directions that they should be worn at all times or there would be consequences.

In July 1938, the Roosevelts again tried to get photographs of FDR with Shirley by inviting her family to a cookout on their estate in Hyde Park, New York. Although the Temples were Republicans and not Roosevelt supporters, they also saw this as solid publicity for ten-year-old Shirley.

Shirley Temple with Eleanor Roosevelt in 1938. –US National Archives and Records Administration

In the movie industry, Shirley was known for being "all business" on the set. However, she was still just a child, and when she arrived on the day of the cookout, Eleanor's grandchildren, Sistie and Buzz Dahl, were not wearing their badges. Shirley asked, "Where are your Shirley Temple Badges?" The children laughed and said they'd left them at their home in Seattle, Washington. Shirley blamed Eleanor, so she had to pay the penalty. Shirley recalled Mrs. Roosevelt "bending over an outdoor grill cooking some hamburgers for us. I was in my little dress with the puffed sleeves and white shoes and had this very feminine lace purse— which contained the slingshot I always carried with me. When I saw Mrs. Roosevelt bending over, I couldn't resist. I hit her with a pebble from my slingshot."

Mrs. Roosevelt straightened up quickly. With the barbecue fork held upright in her hand, she reminded Shirley of the Statue of Liberty. The Secret Service agents assigned to guard the Roosevelts knew something had happened but could not figure out what. Only Shirley's mother saw the prank, but she protected her daughter by remaining silent. Once they returned to their hotel room in New York City, however, Shirley received one of the few spankings in her life. Although she may have had a suspicion, Mrs. Roosevelt never knew for sure what Shirley had done. She sent a cryptic message to Shirley by ending her newspaper column, "My Day," on July 11, 1938, with "A well brought-up, charming child is a joy to all who meet her."

———•••———

Shirley Temple was born on April 23, 1928, in Santa Monica, California. Her father, George, was in the banking business. Her mother, Gertrude, devoted her days to their children: John Stanley (called Jack; born in 1915); George Francis Jr. (known as Sonny; born in 1919); and Shirley. Santa Monica was near the motion picture industry in Hollywood. Movie magazines of the era published articles touting, "Your child should be in pictures!"

Shirley's mother, who had once envisioned having personal fame, decided that her exceptional young daughter could fulfill her dream. Singing and dancing were fun for Shirley, and she liked watching and listening to her mother act out stories, but all of this was serious business to Gertrude, who intended to get Shirley discovered.

Three-year-old Shirley was enrolled in the Meglin Dance Studio in 1931. Ethel Meglin sold the idea to Gertrude by advertising that "dancing also provides an exceptional entrée into the entertainment field, with all its rich rewards." Before each dance lesson, Gertrude would style Shirley's blonde hair into fifty-six ringlets that bounced as she learned the basics of tap, tango, and rumba. A scout from Educational Films Corporation chose her and eleven other boys and girls to play in a series of short comedies called *Baby Burlesks*. Shirley's appearance in these films did not make her an overnight star, however. Her fame began when she was offered a small role in the feature film *Stand Up and Cheer!* by Fox Film Corporation, which merged with Twentieth Century Pictures in 1935. That role led to a contract with that studio and more acting parts. Shirley recalled, "To me [making movies was] always a great big gorgeous game of let's-pretend. Children spend most of their time pretending to be somebody else anyhow. . . . I had a studio full of people to play with me and all the costumes and scenery I needed."

By the time Shirley was five years old in 1934 (in reality she was six—her mother had altered her birth certificate to make her seem younger), she had a short film and two feature films to her credit. During 1934, she acted in nine feature films, including *Bright Eyes*, the first film to be written specifically for her. When asked by a reporter how someone so young learned her lines, Shirley nodded toward her mother and replied, "She reads and reads and reads, and I talk and talk and talk."

Shirley's picture appeared on fourteen magazine covers during her early movie career, and many more articles about her were written in movie magazines, such as *Photoplay*, *Modern Screen*, and

Silver Screen. Sheet music of the songs she sang in the movies, such as "On the Good Ship Lollipop," sold quickly. Look-alike contests were popular—even in foreign countries such as Cuba and Japan. The contest held in Paris, France, in May 1936 had three thousand entries. Mothers named their little girls after her (actress Shirley MacLaine, born in 1934, was one of them) and dressed their daughters in Shirley Temple dresses, coats, and socks. Shirley Temple dolls with hair curled like hers were hot sellers. Shirley's mother once called their family residence in Brentwood "the house a doll built." Other mothers bought products such as Quaker Puffed Wheat because Shirley Temple declared, "This is *my* cereal!" in an ad published in the April 1937 issue of *Ladies' Home Journal.* The Brown Derby restaurant in Hollywood even created a nonalcoholic drink (lemon-lime soda with grenadine and a maraschino cherry) for her that still bears her name. Her brothers teasingly called Shirley "La Temple" for her high-profile status. She could truly be called a "screen veteran" and recognized her fame when she lamented, "I stopped believing in Santa Claus when I was six. Mother took me to see him in a department store and he asked me for my autograph."

Shirley was the top box-office movie star in the United States and worldwide from 1935 to 1938. On February 27, 1935, she was even presented with a miniature Oscar at a time when child stars were not recognized by the Academy of Motion Picture Arts and Sciences. She amused herself during the long evening ceremony by crushing dinner rolls and finally fell asleep at the table. Her parents woke her up to receive the award. Irwin S. Cobb, who presented the Oscar, gushed, "When Santa Claus did you up in a package and dropped you down Creation's chimney, he brought the loveliest Christmas present that I can think of in all the world."

Her fame also made her the main financial provider for her family. Because her mother acted as Shirley's manager, she had a salary in a time when women seldom had high-paying jobs. Shirley's father received raises at the bank where he worked because he brought in customers—Shirley's fans who wanted to associate with her through him.

Making the transition from child star to teen idol is never easy for any actor. The "sparkle" of a dimpled smile and the chubby dancing legs of a toddler may not translate into a teenage heartthrob. So in 1940, Shirley left Twentieth Century Fox Studios, which had made many of her pictures. There is no agreement about whether the studio let her go due to sagging ticket sales for her pictures or whether her parents bought out her contract so she could experience what it was like to be a regular school student. Her mother announced on May 11, 1940, that Shirley would leave "her screen career for the present and will retire to the life of a normal child." Shirley entered Westlake School for Girls in seventh grade, the first time in her life that she was educated in a typical classroom.

Shirley's retirement from motion pictures did not last long, however. She starred in five movies for various studios from 1941 to 1945, but her mind was not completely on her schoolwork or film responsibilities. Her mother had married at seventeen, and Shirley wanted to do the same. Enter John Agar, whom she married in what was called "the wedding of the decade" on September 19, 1945. Although John had never acted, he now decided to give it a try. Shirley and John starred together in *Fort Apache* with John Wayne. John went on to star in other motion pictures, many alongside John Wayne, who became his close friend. On January 30, 1948, Shirley gave birth to their daughter, Linda Susan Agar, but the marriage became rocky after her birth and Shirley filed for divorce on December 5, 1949. After the mandatory one-year waiting period, the divorce became final on December 5, 1950.

In the meantime, a trip to Hawaii changed Shirley's life. In January 1950, she took her parents and daughter there to celebrate the two-year-old's birthday, and she met Charles Alden Black. He remembered, "I really wasn't interested in meeting Shirley Temple. I was living a very full life of my own. . . . I had never seen a Shirley Temple movie." But they had a strong immediate connection and were often together that year. They married on December 16, 1950, just days after Shirley's divorce from John Agar was finalized. Charles, who was from a prominent family, was dropped from the San Francisco Social Register for marrying an actress.

Throughout the spring of 1950, world tensions had arisen over events in Korea, and fighting started in June with the United States supporting South Korea. Charles was in the US Navy Reserve and thought he would be called back to active duty, and in April 1951 he was ordered to report to Washington DC to actively serve again in naval intelligence. Although Shirley had not displayed much interest in politics before, that now changed: "During the two years we were in Washington, I had meant only to get involved in local politics, but of course in Washington local politics are national and international politics."

She gave birth to a son, Charles Alden Black Jr., on April 28, 1952. Shirley liked staying home with her two children; however, because her brother Sonny had developed multiple sclerosis, she volunteered to help raise funds for the National Multiple Sclerosis Society, along with Senator John F. Kennedy (later the thirty-fifth US president), movie star Grace Kelly, and singer Frank Sinatra. When the Korean War ended in 1953, Shirley and her family moved back to California.

After a brief stay in southern California (where Lori Alden Black was born on April 9, 1954), the family moved to Atherton, near San Francisco. From January to December 1958, *Shirley Temple's Storybook* aired on black-and-white television; Shirley narrated sixteen episodes and acted in three. These retellings of classic children's stories were very successful. As one critic noted, "It proved once again that [Shirley Temple] could, if she wanted to, steal Christmas from Tiny Tim." A second season of twenty-five color episodes aired as *The Shirley Temple Show* between September 1960 and July 1961, after which Shirley's active career in show business came to an end. Shirley had starred in fourteen short films, forty-three feature films, and over forty storybook television movies in a career that spanned from 1931 to 1961.

In 1967, Shirley entered a special election in California's eleventh congressional district to fill the seat left vacant by the death of Republican J. Arthur Younger. She hoped to copy the political successes of Californians George Murphy and Ronald Reagan. Murphy had been her dancing partner in the movie *Little Miss Broadway* and was a United States senator (1965–1971). Shirley had starred with Reagan in *That Hagen Girl* in 1947. Reagan was beginning his first of two terms as California governor (1967–1975) and would later be elected president of the United States. Shirley ran as a conservative and emphasized four issues in her speeches: (1) escalating the Vietnam War so it would end quickly; (2) ending crime in the streets; (3) reducing taxes for homeowners; and (4) stopping the spread of pornography. The famous singer Bing Crosby (who belonged to the same golf club as Shirley's husband, Charles) hosted a hundred-dollar-a-plate dinner fundraiser for her. Called "A Party with Shirley," it received national attention, but that wasn't enough. Shirley lost the primary election to Pete McCloskey, a law school professor and liberal Republican who was an outspoken opponent of the Vietnam War. In her consolation speech, Shirley said, "I will be back. I am dedicating my life to public service because the country needs us now more than ever before and I want to help."

On August 29, 1969, President Richard Nixon named Shirley as a member of the US delegation to the Twenty-Fourth General Assembly of the United Nations. She spoke out about the problems of the aged, the plight of refugees worldwide, and environmental issues.

In the early 1970s, health issues for women were kept private—especially for famous people. Shirley broke that tradition when she had a mastectomy in 1972. Speaking from her hospital bed in San Francisco about what she had undergone, she pioneered breast cancer awareness for women. The public response was extremely positive: she received fifty thousand letters in a week and numerous bouquets of flowers. After her announcement, the American Cancer Society reported a 30 percent increase in women seeking information about self-examination for breast cancer. While many years would pass before October would be designated Breast Cancer Awareness Month in 1985 and the Susan G. Komen Race for the Cure would become the largest nonprofit source of funding for the fight against breast cancer, Shirley truly led the way for their creation.

President Gerald R. Ford appointed Shirley US ambassador to Ghana in 1974, a position she held until 1976. Her work in the United Nations had given her insight into Africa and its people. Once asked about her appointment, Ford replied, "Ghana was a very upward African nation during that continent's turmoil in the 1970s. It was important that the new ambassador be identified as a personal choice of the White House. Mrs. Black was so recognized. Her appointment was a clear indication of presidential concern in Africa."

Learning to be an ambassador was not easy. In the ten weeks before she left for Ghana, Shirley attended fifty-five official state briefings about the country. Her ultimate arrival was filmed by the American television program *60 Minutes*. Shirley vividly remembered the moment when she was presented to the head of the country, Kwame Nkrumah: "It was probably the most thrilling moment of my life. Standing alone in a little canopied setting with the Ghanaian Air Force band playing 'The Star-Spangled Banner' was almost too much. I was covered in gooseflesh; then the talking drums of welcome really covered me in gooseflesh. . . . To me it was like the *National Geographic* magazine come to life."

Shirley had two goals while in Ghana: promote American business interests and encourage the US government and people to help with the economic development of African countries. The local people appreciated the fact that she often wore colorful

Shirley Temple Black with President Gerald Ford on July 20, 1976.
–White House Photographic Office Collection

African dresses when she participated in activities. Ghana was a matriarchal society, which also helped people accept her as a leader. One year during her term, Shirley wanted to highlight American customs to the guests invited to a formal Fourth of July celebration. Besides hot dogs, potato salad, and corn on the cob, she ordered peanut butter and jelly sandwiches. In the buffet line, guests were puzzled by the trays of a soupy green mixture that covered some type of squares. The kitchen staff had used green gelatin (like Jell-O), which to them was jelly. It melted in the heat and caused the bizarre-looking food. The guests just thought it was a typical American dish. Shirley learned she had to be very specific with her requests.

At the end of her term as ambassador, President Ford requested that she become the chief of protocol of the United States. The first woman ever to hold that position in the State Department, she was sworn in on July 20, 1976. She oversaw a staff of almost fifty people and her duties were extremely varied, but the position lasted only six months; when Jimmy Carter was elected, she was replaced. However, she was the one in charge of the arrangements for Carter's inauguration and the official inaugural ball.

Under President George H. W. Bush, Shirley was appointed ambassador to Czechoslovakia (1989–1992), the first female ambassador to that country. The Czech president in power when she arrived, Gustáv Husák, had been a fan of "Shirleyka," and they established a good working relationship because of her films. She witnessed the overthrow of the Communist government in that country and ended her assignment just as the country was splitting into the Czech Republic and Slovakia in 1992.

During her dual career in the film industry and politics, Shirley was recognized for her achievements in many ways. On January 1, 1977, she received the Life Achievement Award of the American Center for Films for Children. On May 20, 1985, the Academy Foundation of the Academy of Motion Picture Arts and Sciences honored her with "A Tribute to Shirley Temple" evening and presented her with a full-size Oscar to replace the miniature one she had been given in 1935. On the American Film Institute's list of the fifty greatest screen legends, Shirley ranks eighteenth out of the twenty-five female stars listed. The list was unveiled on June 15, 1999, in a CBS television special that Shirley hosted. She was also the recipient of Kennedy Center Honors (1998) and a Screen Actors Guild Life Achievement Award (2005). A life-size bronze statue of her as a child, by sculptor Nijel Binns, has welcomed other actors to the Fox Studios lot since 2002.

On November 23, 1987, Shirley was recognized by US Secretary of State George P. Schulz as an honorary foreign service officer. The citation states, "In recognition of your distinguished contributions to the diplomacy of the country you have so ably represented at home and abroad, and with grateful appreciation for your willingness to share your experiences, insights and wisdom in the training of virtually every first-time ambassador appointed since January 20, 1981."

Shirley also received honorary degrees from Santa Clara University, Lehigh University, and the College of Notre Dame. She always accepted the accolades with grace. She once noted, "I've been so blessed. If someone asked me whom I would choose to be if I could come back in another life, I would have to say Shirley Temple Black. I cannot think of a more interesting life to ask for."

Charles Black died in 2005. Shirley followed him on February 10, 2014, at her home in Woodside, California. Although it was first reported that she died of natural causes, it was later revealed that she died from pneumonia compounded by chronic obstructive pulmonary disease (COPD) caused by cigarette smoking. Although she had boasted about being a chain-smoker as a teenager, she had tried to keep the habit a secret as an adult so she would be a positive role model for children and her fans.

Her fame endures, kept alive by Shirley Temple fan clubs, as well as collectors' groups and makers of dolls and memorabilia. Her personal collection of items from her childhood years (1928–1940), which her mother collected, became a traveling museum exhibition in select cities from New York to California starting on April 30, 2015. Entitled "Love, Shirley Temple," it ended with an auction held at the historic Little Theatre in Kansas City, Missouri, on July 14, 2015. Shirley's family stated that "these artifacts should now be shared across the world with collectors, fans, and museums as tangible reminders of this child-star's irrepressibly joyful and optimistic persona." People who want an inside look at her life as a film star can read her 1988 autobiography, *Child Star*.

In 2016, the US Postal Service created the Shirley Temple Forever Stamp, the twentieth inductee into the Postal Service's "Legends of Hollywood" series. The picture of her is based on a painting by Tim O'Brien from her 1935 movie *Curly Top*.

Shirley Temple Black was like that Forever postage stamp. The varied ways she supported our nation will never lose their value, and her name will be known forever.

Civil rights advocate Dolores Huerta speaking at an event in Phoenix, Arizona, in March 2016.
–Photographed by Gage Skidmore

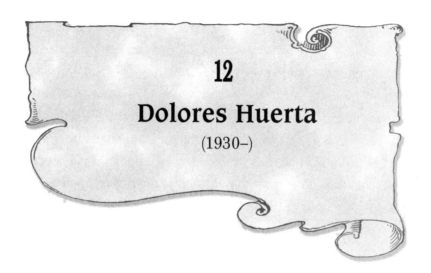

12
Dolores Huerta
(1930–)

Discrimination Fighter

Dolores Huerta had nothing against grapes. But she refused to eat them. She also didn't want anyone else in the United States or around the world to purchase or consume grapes either. Since about eleven million people were buying them, Dolores knew she had a big task ahead of her. If she succeeded, that would be an impressive feat for a slight, barely five-foot-two-inch Hispanic woman.

Why did Dolores feel this way? Grapes were a major farm crop in California in the 1960s, and starting in the fall of 1965 table grapes became the focal point in the struggles of the farm workers in California. Grape pickers around Delano (near Bakersfield at the southern end of the Central Valley) had walked out of the vineyards and refused to harvest the ripening fruit to protest poor wages and working conditions. During the grape strike, the farm workers used various tactics to get their voices heard. In addition to consumer boycotts, they organized nonviolent resistance, such as picketing and protest marches. On March 17, 1966, sixty-eight workers and two leaders started a march of over two hundred miles, from Delano to Sacramento, in order to draw attention to their cause and put pressure on the growers. Dolores Huerta was one of the leaders; César Chávez was the other. The marchers carrying protest signs considered themselves *peregrinos* (pilgrims), trying to get their message out to the world. Voices shouted over and over, *"Viva la Huelga!"* (Long live the strike!) They were harassed by local police and had many long days of walking, traveling about fifteen miles each day. But people continued to join the march. By the time they arrived in Stockton, about 1,500 people were involved, not including the press, FBI agents, and curious onlookers.

It worked.

On March 25, even before the marchers reached Sacramento, the Schenley Wine Company agreed to a contract with the National Farm Workers Association that improved workers' pay and working conditions. This was the first time in US history that a major corporation recognized a collective bargaining agreement (labor contract) negotiated by the workers themselves. The marchers continued and celebrated their success at the state capitol building on Easter Sunday, April 10, 1966. Fifty-one of the original marchers made it the whole way. They were joined by around ten thousand people who had gathered and heard the good news about the settlement from César Chávez that day. Dolores created the actual contract that was signed. On the fiftieth anniversary of this event, Dolores recalled, "When we started the march to Sacramento there were 70 people striking. We ended up at 10,000 people. It doesn't take an army [to make a difference], just a committed few."

She and the other marchers still alive in 2016 (as well as surviving family members of those who were deceased) received letters from US Labor Secretary Thomas Perez. He praised their roles in the march: "Your example inspired generations of reformers who came after you to summon the moral courage that it takes to put one's own life and livelihood on the line for something greater."

But this one event did not remedy the plight of the farm workers. It took years to gain improvements across the state, and Dolores was right in the middle of the struggle every day.

———•••———

Dolores Clara Fernández was born on April 10, 1930, in Dawson, New Mexico, a small mining town. Her mother, Alicia Margaret Chávez, was second-generation New Mexican. Her father, Juan Fabán Fernández, had been born in Dawson, but his parents were Mexican immigrants. Dolores's father started out as a farm laborer and miner. He became a union activist who ran for political office and was elected a state assemblyman in the New Mexico legislature in 1938. The couple divorced when Dolores was three years old.

Dolores spent most of her childhood and early adult life in Stockton, California, where she and her two brothers, John and Marshal, moved with their mother. Dolores once described her mother as "a Mexican American Horatio Alger type." (Horatio Alger was an American writer who penned stories about teenagers working hard to escape poverty.) Alicia Fernández worked as a waitress by day and in a cannery at night while Dolores's grandfather, Herculano Chávez, watched the children. Although Alicia remarried, she and James Richards quickly divorced. Alicia got to keep the hotel they ran (Richards' Hotel), and she later leased the Center Hotel. Dolores and her brothers helped out at these establishments, which were popular with working-class and farm worker clientele. Alicia was independent and ambitious, and she also had a kind heart. She often let people stay even if they couldn't pay. Alicia also made sure Dolores and her brothers shared equally in household chores such as cooking and doing laundry. Dolores was not taught to take care of the males, as was the norm in many families of the era. In addition, Alicia was an active member of the local community and was involved in numerous civic organizations as well as the church. Dolores credits her mother as being extremely important in how she led her life. She once commented, "My mother was my greatest influence. Ever since I was a little girl, my mother would tell me, 'If you see something that needs to be done, you have to do it for yourself.'"

Stockton was a diverse community, so Dolores learned early to get along with people from varied backgrounds. As she described it, "The ethnic community where we lived was all mixed. It was Japanese, Chinese. The only Jewish families that lived in Stockton were there in our neighborhood. . . . There was the Filipino pool hall . . . , the Mexican drug stores, the Mexican bakeries were there."

Dolores had a busy childhood. She became a Girl Scout when she was eight and stayed a Scout until she was eighteen, took piano and violin lessons, danced flamenco, marched in the school band, and sang in the choir. To earn money as a teenager, she worked in a fruit cannery. She liked to write and was dismayed when in her senior year of high school, an English teacher thought someone else had written her essays because they were so well expressed. This brush with prejudice would remain a vivid memory for her.

Graduating from Stockton High School in 1947, Dolores immediately enrolled in Delta Community College (now known as San Joaquin Delta Community College). In 1948, she abandoned her studies and married her high school sweetheart, Ralph Head, with whom she had two daughters, Celeste (born July 27, 1950) and Lori Edith (born June 28, 1952). The marriage ended in 1953, and she returned to college, where she earned an associate teaching credential. But Dolores soon realized that she wasn't cut out to be a teacher. She explained, "I couldn't stand seeing kids come to class hungry and needing shoes. I thought I could do more by organizing farm workers than by trying to teach their hungry children."

So Dolores became a community organizer trying to get the parents of her former students their basic human rights. In 1955, she was a founding member of the Stockton Community Service Organization (CSO), where she set up voter registration drives and lobbied local governments to improve the neighborhoods where farm workers lived. She also joined the Agricultural Workers Association (AWA), which had been created by a local priest and his congregation. Through the AWA, she lobbied politicians to give migrant workers who weren't US citizens the ability to get public assistance and pensions. She also successfully pushed legislation that allowed Spanish-speaking voters the right to vote on ballots written in Spanish and to take driver's license examinations in their native language. AWA later merged with the Agricultural Workers Organizing Committee to become the United Farm Workers Organizing Committee.

During the course of all of these activities, Dolores met and married Ventura P. Huerta on December 30, 1955. In Spanish, Dolores means "sorrow" and Huerta "orchard," so now her name seemed somewhat of a reflection of her work. Ventura was also involved in community work. The couple had five children together, but the marriage ended in 1961. Ventura wanted a traditional stay-at-home wife, so they often argued over Dolores's efforts to juggle domestic tasks, child care, and her work in social activism. As she noted, "I knew I wasn't comfortable in a wife's role, but I wasn't clearly facing the issue. I hedged, I made excuses, I didn't come out and tell my husband that I cared more about helping other people than cleaning our house and doing my hair."

Through her CSO activities, Dolores met César Chávez in 1956. The two quickly discovered that they shared a common desire to organize farm workers into a union. But this idea was not part of the mission of the CSO. Consequently, César and Dolores resigned from that organization in the spring of 1962 and created a workers' union called the National Farm Workers Association (NFWA), which became the United Farm Workers (UFW) in August 1966. While César became the public face and speaker for the organization, Dolores has been called the hidden leader. Her organizing skills were a key factor in the growth of the group.

Being an educated Mexican woman in this time period, she had to deal with discrimination at times, which was challenging. But she was devoted to her work (the farm workers called her *La Pasionaria*, "The Passionate One") and confident in her abilities. In one of her letters to César, she joked, "Being a now (ahem) experienced lobbyist, I am able to speak on a man-to-man basis with other lobbyists." Those she negotiated with did not view this skill favorably. One grower complained, saying, "Dolores Huerta is crazy. She is a violent woman, where women, especially Mexican women, are usually peaceful and calm."

In 1963, her tough lobbying and negotiation abilities secured California farm workers money from the Aid for Dependent Families program and disability insurance. Her successes were pulling farm workers and their families into NFWA. In 1965, the Filipino grape pickers demanded pay equal to the federal minimum wage standard by going on strike. NFWA joined their cause on September 16, 1965; that date was chosen because it was Mexican Independence Day. Dolores helped organize the strike of over five thousand grape workers, which came to be known as the Delano Grape Strike. It wasn't an easy time for those who were involved. The growers used farm equipment to spray dust all over the strikers. They were also covered with bug poison, attacked by dogs, called a lot of insulting names, and sometimes beaten. Some growers just brought in new workers to take their jobs. Dolores was not immune to these attacks, and the worst in her career came even later. In September 1988, while she was protesting outside the St. Francis Hotel in San Francisco against what she perceived to be the pro-war and antiworker policies of George H. W. Bush, who was on the campaign trail to be elected US president, a police officer broke four of her ribs and shattered her spleen with his baton. Because the beating was caught on videotape, it was aired heavily on local television news stations. The public was outraged. Dolores was awarded an out-of-court settlement, which was used for the benefit of farm workers. This incident forced the San Francisco Police Department to change its regulations regarding crowd control and how police officers were disciplined.

While the farm workers lacked finances to support their cause (Dolores received a salary of $10 per week), they did make a significant voting bloc in California. Robert F. Kennedy acknowledged Dolores's help in winning the 1968 California Democratic Presidential Primary. She stood beside him on the platform at the Ambassador Hotel in Los Angeles on June 5, 1968, as he delivered his victory speech. Only moments later, Dolores was walking behind Kennedy as he and five other people were shot inside the hotel's kitchen pantry. She was not hurt, but Kennedy died from his gunshot wounds the next day. This event did not deter Dolores.

On May 10, 1969, which was set as International Boycott Day, she proclaimed:

> We, the striking grape workers of California, join on this International Boycott Day with the consumers across the continent in planning the steps that lie ahead on the road to our liberation. . . . Grapes must remain an unenjoyed luxury for all as long as the barest human needs and basic human rights are still luxuries for farm workers. The grapes grow sweet and heavy on the vines, but they will have to wait while we reach out first for our freedom. The time is ripe for our liberation.

Dolores's words, in what is known as the Proclamation of the Delano Grape Workers, convinced some chain grocery stores not to stock grapes and some consumers not to buy grapes. Since New York City was the primary distribution point for table grapes on the East Coast, Dolores left California to become the boycott coordinator at that site. She knew she had to reach beyond the Hispanic community for the boycott to be successful, so she rallied many groups to join the cause. These included other labor unions, political activists, community associations, church organizations, student clubs, and concerned people from across many racial, ethnic, and class configurations. She made people aware of the deplorable working conditions of the workers in the fields as well as their low rate of pay and exposure to harmful toxics. Child labor was a common practice, and those working in fields had no drinking water or toilets. Dolores kept media attention focused on their cause. To do that, she sometimes wore a T-shirt that said "There's Blood on those Grapes." At one point, more than fourteen million Americans stopped buying grapes as a way to support the striking workers.

It took until July 29, 1970, for the UFW to reach a contract agreement with twenty-six table-grape growers, which by then affected over ten thousand farm workers. It had taken five years to get these growers to agree to contracts that provided fair wages as well as health and benefit plans for the workers. Reflecting on this later, Dolores observed, "I think we brought to the world, the United States anyway, the whole idea of boycotting as a nonviolent tactic. I think we showed the world that nonviolence can work to make social change. . . . I think we have laid a pattern of how farmworkers are eventually going to get out of bondage."

Dolores recalled that when she was a child, her maternal grandfather called her "seven tongues . . . because I always talked so much." He noted that she had plenty to say and was never shy about making her opinions known. Obviously, this verbal talent was an important factor in achieving this success for the farm workers.

Unfortunately, many growers didn't honor the agreements they made. So in 1973, Dolores led another consumer boycott, which resulted in the 1975 passage of the California Agricultural Labor Relations Law. It granted California farm workers the right to collectively organize and negotiate for better wages and working conditions.

Dolores continued to lobby for workers' rights with other agricultural growers over the years. She became close to Richard

Chávez, César's younger brother. Together they fought for workers' rights and established a personal relationship that produced four children—Juana, Ricky, Maria Elena, and Camilia.

Although Dolores has followed a nontraditional lifestyle, she initially regarded the women's liberation movement of the 1960s as not pertaining to her. She considered it to be a "middle-class phenomenon." However, after meeting Gloria Steinem, a leader in the women's movement, she realized that their views meshed more than she had previously imagined. Dolores began to challenge gender discrimination within the farm workers' movement. One day at a meeting, she decided to write down every insulting comment about women she heard spoken. At the end, she told the men in the group that she had heard fifty-eight sexist remarks. Many were surprised—they were unaware that what they were saying was rude. Dolores did the same thing at the next meeting. This time, she counted thirty sexist comments. By speaking up and bringing to the men's awareness the fact that both men and women need to be treated in a courteous manner, Dolores was changing their behavior.

Dolores continued her activist work after César Chávez died on April 23, 1993, although she resigned from the UFW in 2000. In 2002, she led a 265-mile march from Bakersfield to Sacramento in the grueling heat of a California summer in order to get Governor Gray Davis to support legislation that would benefit farm workers. He signed the legislation on September 30, 2002. In a letter to Dolores, he called her his "conscience." In December of that year, Dolores was awarded the Puffin/Nation Prize for Creative Citizenship, an award given annually to an "individual who has challenged the status quo through distinctive, courageous, imaginative and socially responsible work of significance." She used the $100,000 that came with the honor to create a nonprofit foundation in Bakersfield to train activists (especially Latinas) to continue what she had begun. The mission of the Dolores Huerta Foundation is to "create a network of organized healthy communities pursuing social justice through systemic and structural transformation."

Dolores has received much recognition for her life's work. In 1984, the California state senate gave her the Outstanding Labor Leader Award. In 1993, she was inducted into the National Women's Hall of Fame, presented the Roger Baldwin Medal of Liberty Award from the American Civil Liberties Union, and given the Ellis Island Medal of Freedom Award and the Eugene V. Debs Foundation Outstanding American Award. The following year, she was presented with the Woman of Courage Award from the National Organization of Women. That same year, 1994, Ben & Jerry's ice cream company gave her free ice cream for life for her participation (along with seven other activists) in their socially oriented ad campaign. *Ms.* magazine named her one of the three most important women of 1997, and President Bill Clinton gave her the Eleanor D. Roosevelt Human Rights Award the following year. In 2001, she was presented the Smithsonian Institution's James Smithson Award for being someone who has made "distinguished contributions to the advancement of areas of interest to the Smithsonian." In 2011, she received the Icons of the American Civil Rights Movement Award, as part of the Martin Luther King Jr. Awards, from the National Association for the Advancement of Colored People.

Probably the most prestigious of all of her awards was bestowed in 2012 by President Barack Obama. She was presented the Presidential Medal of Freedom, the highest civilian award in the United States. Upon receiving this award, Dolores said:

> The freedom of association means that people can come together in organization to fight for solutions to the problems they confront in their communities. The great social justice changes in our country have happened when people came together, organized, and took direct action. It is this right that sustains and nurtures our democracy today. The civil rights movement, the labor movement, the women's movement, and the equality movement for our LGBT

brothers and sisters are all manifestations of these rights. I thank President Obama for raising the importance of organizing to the highest level of merit and honor.

But that wasn't the end of recognition for Dolores. She was inducted into the California Hall of Fame in March of 2013. She holds nine honorary doctorate degrees from universities throughout the country. Although her career as a teacher was brief, she has served as a regent for the University of California system, and there are four elementary schools in California (Los Angeles, Stockton, Lennox, and Fontana), one in Fort Worth, Texas, and a high school in Pueblo, Colorado, named for her. In 2015, it was announced that a documentary film would be made about her life. One of the movie's producers was Grammy Award–winning musician Carlos Santana (also in the Ben & Jerry's ad of 1994). The film, *Dolores*, was released in 2017 at the Sundance Film Festival and includes what Dolores is very proud of: her eleven children. Following their mother's motto (which she devised for the UFW) of *"Si se puede"*–"Yes, it can be done"–her children have taken career paths as a doctor, a nurse, a lawyer, an artist, business executives, health care workers, youth program coordinators, and, of course, organizers. One of her daughters heads the Dolores Huerta Foundation. From July 3, 2015, to May 15, 2016, an exhibit entitled "One Life: Dolores Huerta" was featured at the National Portrait Gallery in Washington DC. The opening day marked the fiftieth anniversary of the September 16, 1965, grape strike launched by the farm workers' movement.

Even after decades of social reform efforts on a very bumpy road (by age seventy, she had been arrested twenty-two times, most often for not obeying antipicketing orders), Dolores still works as an advocate for the working poor, women, and children. She has stated that she would like to be remembered "as a woman who cares for fellow humans. We must use our lives to make the world a better place to live, not just acquire things. That is what we are put on Earth for." There is a *corrido* (narrative song popular in Mexico) about Dolores Huerta. Sung by the rock band Los Lobos, it begins:

> In Dawson, New Mexico
>
> The April 10
>
> Dolores Huerta was born
>
> Nobody imagined
>
> That she would go head
>
> Part of the great movement

But one person did imagine that: Dolores Huerta. How could she fail when she believed *"Si se puede"*?

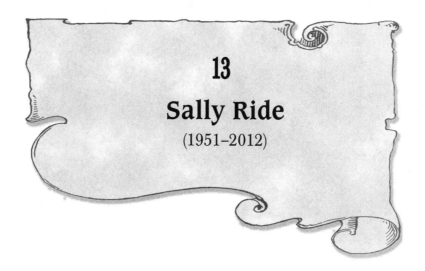

13

Sally Ride

(1951–2012)

FIRST AMERICAN WOMAN IN SPACE

Making a peanut butter sandwich is easy: Slap peanut butter over one slice of bread and then cover it with another piece of bread and the sandwich is ready to eat. Right? Sally Ride used to think that was it. However, in 1983, she learned it was much harder when you are in space!

On Earth, it takes only one person to make a peanut butter sandwich. In space, it takes three. One person holds the peanut butter jar and the lid—they can't be put down or they'll float away in the weightlessness of space. Sally would throw the lid to another astronaut if she was making the sandwich. Then she would pick up the knife and load it with peanut butter. Another person had to get the bread out and hold it so Sally could spread the peanut butter on it. That person also added the top slice of bread. Finally, the sandwich was ready. Sally advised eating it fast, before it floated away!

Sticky foods are the easiest to eat in space. They stay put and don't float away. But astronauts also eat freeze-dried and vacuum-packed foods. That way they can also enjoy soup, vegetables, and different kinds of casseroles while traveling in space. For

Sally Ride in space. –National Aeronautics and Space Administration

example, one meal could be hot dogs, macaroni and cheese, and lemonade, with cookies for dessert. Peanuts were an easy snack. Each person has a knife, fork, and spoon, but the spoon and a pair of scissors were actually the most useful eating utensils because the foil packages many foods are cooked in must be cut open. The contents can be spooned into the mouth. If a blob of food (for example, pudding) gets away, it has to be caught before it hits a wall. Usually one astronaut prepares the meal for the whole crew. Sally did not especially like to cook as part of her life on Earth. How did she get into a situation where she was cooking in space?

—— ••• ——

Sally Kristen Ride was born on May 26, 1951, in Los Angeles, California. On that day, the *Saturday Evening Post* published a short article titled "Smart Girls Are Helpless." Its message was that women needed to act dependent and needy in order to succeed in a man's world. Luckily, Sally's parents, Dale and Joyce Ride, didn't believe that. They let Sally and her younger sister, Karen (usually called Bear), try all kinds of things. In 1983, when their mother was interviewed by *People* magazine, she stated, "Dale and I simply forgot to tell them that there were things they couldn't do. But I think if it had occurred to us to tell them, we would have refrained." It was probably a wise move because Sally was headstrong and independent, even as a child.

The Ride family lived in Encino. Dr. Ride was a professor of political science at Santa Monica Community College. Sally's mother remained at home with the children when they were young, but later she taught English to foreign students. Both parents were active in the Presbyterian Church.

Sally knew how to read by age five. Each day, she would race her father for the sports section of the newspaper. She was passionate about sports and would memorize the statistics for various sports teams from the newspaper reports. Sally was also very athletic and hoped to play baseball for the Los Angeles Dodgers one day!

When Sally was nine, Sally's father took a sabbatical leave from his position, and the family traveled around Europe, greatly expanding Sally's view of the world. Upon their return home, her mother got Sally interested in playing tennis, a more structured and less dangerous sport than the street football in which Sally often participated. Sally began playing tennis against her father, but he quickly realized she was much better than he was. At age eleven, Sally became a student of Alice Marble, a former tennis champion and renowned teacher. Alice found Sally to be a perfectionist and once commented that "she had talent, a lot of athletic ability. But she seemed so frustrated with it." But Sally did well and was soon a nationally ranked player on the junior tennis circuit. Athletic scholarships came her way, and she accepted a partial scholarship to Westlake School for Girls, a highly celebrated school in Los Angeles.

Sally met and became friends with Susan Okie, who remembered her at that time as "a fleet-footed 14-year-old with keen blue eyes, a self-confident grin, and long straight hair that perpetually flopped forward over her face." Sally continued to play tennis at the school, becoming team captain her senior year, but her studies also deepened her interest in math and science. Sally once stated, "Math and science were always my favorite subjects in school. I was pestering my parents for chemistry sets and telescopes and that sort of thing." They also gifted her with a subscription to *Scientific American* magazine.

After graduating from Westlake in 1968, Sally attended Swarthmore College outside Philadelphia, Pennsylvania, for three semesters. She declared a major in physics and continued to play tennis. But Sally missed the West Coast and wanted to play tennis more. As she recalled, "I thought I was quitting college to play tennis. And then I realized after a month or so back in California that it wasn't the smartest thing to be doing."

She applied and was accepted to Stanford University in Palo Alto, California, near San Francisco. The school had a highly rated women's tennis team as well as a solid academic reputation. One of few women in the physics program, Sally eventually stopped playing tennis so she could concentrate on her studies. She also discovered Shakespeare. To Sally, reading Shakespeare's works was like solving a puzzle: "You had to figure out what he was trying to say and find all the little clues inside the play that you were right." Since Sally had loved reading Nancy Drew and Ian Fleming's James Bond books when she was young, it is no wonder that she found Shakespeare fascinating. Sally graduated from Stanford in 1973 with a bachelor of science degree in physics and a bachelor of arts degree in English.

Sally opted to continue her studies, entering graduate school at Stanford in physics. Her specific area of study was in astrophysics—exploring how free electrons behaved in a magnetic field. She completed a master's degree in physics in 1975 and was close to finishing her PhD in 1977. One day, she happened to read an ad in the campus newspaper: The National Aeronautics and Space

Administration (NASA) was accepting applications for astronauts. NASA was looking for scientists to serve as mission specialists and to supervise experiments during space flights. Sally recalled, "The moment I saw that, I knew that's what I wanted to do. I wanted to apply to the astronaut corps and see whether NASA would take me, and see whether I could have the opportunity to go on that adventure."

The applicants to be an astronaut included 1,544 women and 6,535 men. After multiple screenings, 200 finalists (in groups of 20) were brought to the Johnson Space Center in Houston, Texas, for a week of interviews, tests, and briefings. Sally's group went in October 1977. In 1983, Sally told *Ms.* magazine that "nobody knew what to expect. From what we'd heard and read, we thought they'd put us in centrifuges, dunk us in ice water, hang us up by our toes, anything!" During her time at the Johnson Space Center, Sally was subjected to a wide variety of examinations, but she wasn't hung upside down. At the end of the week, she returned to Stanford to continue her PhD studies.

On January 16, 1978, the phone rang. Sally was notified that she had been accepted as a space shuttle astronaut. Of the thirty-five individuals accepted, only six were women. She was thrilled and recalled, "I thought maybe I was dreaming. . . . My biggest frustration was that it was five or six in the morning in California, so all my friends and family were asleep. I wasn't sure that I should wake them up to give them the news!"

NASA held a press conference that day in Washington DC to introduce the new astronaut candidates—known as AsCans. Stanford University was also proud of Sally's selection and held its own press conference to honor her achievement.

Two weeks later, Sally met all of the AsCans at an orientation meeting. There were three African American men and one Japanese American male candidate as well as the other Caucasian men. Sally learned that the other women had varied backgrounds, including a geologist, an electrical engineer, a surgeon, a chemist, and a biochemist. One was Kathryn Sullivan, who noted in 2007 that the media focused on the women and minority men. She quipped, "We eventually came to refer to our class as 'ten interesting people and twenty-five standard white guys.'"

Before her training began, Sally was able to return to Stanford and finish her PhD in 1978. Her dissertation was titled *The Interaction of X-Rays with the Interstellar Medium*. During her research, Sally never imagined she would soon see the latter (the gas and dust between the stars) up close.

Part of her training to become an astronaut included learning to fly an airplane. Sally commented, "The flying was totally foreign to me and an awful lot of fun. I really enjoyed both the ground school and then flight training itself." Sally's assignment with NASA was to help develop the shuttle's robot arm, which was officially called the Shuttle Remote Manipulator System. Because it was being built in Toronto, Canada, much of Sally's time was spent there. Sally explained, "The robot arm was designed to move materials such as satellites in and out of the space shuttle's cargo bay." Any mistake could be costly in terms of the shuttle itself or people's lives. Sally had to try to imagine everything that could possibly go wrong with the robot arm and write instructions on how to fix those problems. She completed her training as a mission specialist in 1979.

On April 19, 1982, Sally was informed that she would soon be going into space. That may have motivated her to get married, which she did on July 24, 1982. Her new husband was fellow astronaut Steven Alan Hawley. Sally piloted her own plane to Steven's parents' house in Kansas, where she got married wearing jeans and a rugby shirt. Since her sister Bear was now a Presbyterian minister, she married the couple. They moved into a house near Johnson Space Center, adorning their walls with posters and photographs of jet airplanes, space shuttles, and the logo designed for their astronaut class. Neither liked to cook, and they ate a lot of potato chips and probably peanut butter sandwiches.

On June 18, 1983, Sally became the first American woman to orbit Earth when she blasted off from Kennedy Space Center near Cape Canaveral, Florida, and flew aboard Space Shuttle *Challenger*. At thirty-two years of age, she was also the youngest person in space at that time. Sally felt the pressure: "It came with a lot of responsibility. I was very aware through the training that I needed to understand my job well enough and perform it well enough in space that I wouldn't cast doubt on whether women should be in the astronaut corps."

Sally stayed in space for six days. One of her jobs was to test the robotic arm by putting a satellite into space. All of her training paid off. She successfully launched the satellite!

Her second flight was also aboard *Challenger* in 1984, and the mission lasted eight days. With this flight, Sally became the only woman ever to travel in space twice. She was slated to fly a third mission on Space Shuttle *Challenger* around July 1986, but it never happened. On January 28, 1986, Sally was on a commercial airline heading back to Houston when the pilot announced that there had been an accident with space shuttle mission STS-51-L, the *Challenger*'s tenth. The seven astronauts aboard had all been killed, including Christa McAuliffe, the high school teacher who was part of the crew. President Ronald Reagan appointed the thirteen members of the Rogers Commission to investigate the causes of the Space Shuttle *Challenger* disaster. Sally was selected to be a member of the commission. She was the only active astronaut and the only woman on that team. It was a difficult time for her, as she related, "I was just going from day to day and just grinding through all the data that we had to grind through. But it was a very, very difficult time. . . . It was very, very hard on all of us. You could see it in our faces in the months that followed the accident."

The Rogers Commission Report revealed that there had been a problem with the O-rings on the solid rocket booster. Sally also served on the disaster review board that investigated the loss of

Space Shuttle *Columbia* in 2003, being the only expert to participate in exploring both tragedies.

Although Sally had been slated to fly again, she left NASA in 1987 to become a teacher at Stanford University, her alma mater. She also divorced her husband in May of that year. In 1989, she switched to the University of California, San Diego, where she became a professor of physics and director of the California Space Institute, remaining there until 1996.

Sally had always been interested in getting young people to pursue careers in science, technology, engineering, and math (known as STEM). During her NASA days, she traveled with fellow astronauts to speak to high school and college students on a monthly basis. Sally always remembered how much she had enjoyed the lessons of Dr. Elizabeth Mommaerts at Westlake School. From Dr. Mommaerts, Sally had learned the scientific method. With her childhood friend Susan Okie, who had became a journalist with the *Washington Post*, Sally coauthored a book titled *To Space and Back*, published in 1986, in which she shared "her personal experience of traveling into space" for a juvenile audience. Sally dedicated this book to Dr. Mommaerts and the lost crew of the *Challenger*.

Sally also coauthored some books for young readers with Tam O'Shaughnessy, another longtime friend from her days in tennis. These included *The Mystery of Mars* (1999), *The Third Planet: Exploring the Earth from Space* (1994), *Voyager: An Adventure to the Edge of the Solar System* (1992), and *Mission: Planet Earth: Our World and Its Climate—and How Humans Are Changing Them* (2009). Sally and Tam formed a strong bond through their common interest in education and became life partners.

In 2000, Sally worked with NASA to start EarthKAM, an Internet-based effort that allowed middle school students to shoot and download photos of Earth from space. The following year, she founded an organization named Imaginary Lines. Its mission was "to increase the number of girls who are technically literate and who have the foundation they need to go on in science, math or

Former astronaut Sally Ride speaking to the media prior to an astronomy demonstration on the lawn of the White House in Washington DC on October 7, 2009. −Associated Press photo/Pablo Martinez Monsivais

engineering." Sally Ride Science evolved from this. Girls attended summer camps and other programs to learn about science and technology. Part of this was the Sally Ride Science Clubs. In these locally based groups, girls met others with similar interests and participated in a range of activities. The Sally Ride Science Junior Academy started annually in 2016. Weeklong workshops are held near San Diego, where girls engage in STEAM (science, technology, engineering, art, and mathematics) activities. Sally Ride Science is now a nonprofit organization run by the University of California, San Diego.

As one of the few people who have seen Earth from space, Sally received much recognition. Her commitment to educating the young about space earned her the Jefferson Award from the American Institute for Public Service in 1984. Sally was inducted into the International Space Hall of Fame in 1985 and the National Women's Hall of Fame in 1988. She was the first woman inducted into the US Astronaut Hall of Fame (2003). Sally also received the 2005 Theodore Roosevelt Award from the National Collegiate Athletic Association (NCAA), an award presented to a graduate of an NCAA institution whose experiences as a varsity athlete were a springboard to "a distinguished career of national significance and achievement." In 2006, Sally was inducted into the California Hall of Fame. She also was twice awarded the NASA Space Flight Medal in recognition of her time in space.

Sally stopped making public appearances in 2011. Always a private person, Sally did not tell many people that it was because she had pancreatic cancer. After a seventeen-month battle with the disease, she died on July 23, 2012, in La Jolla, California, at age sixty-one and was buried at Woodlawn Memorial Cemetery in Santa Monica, California. President Barack Obama noted about her passing that "Sally was a national hero and a powerful role model. Sally's life showed us that there are no limits to what we can achieve, and I have no doubt that her legacy will endure for years to come." In 2013, President Obama posthumously awarded

Sally the Presidential Medal of Freedom, one of the highest civilian awards in the United States. A national tribute called "Sally Ride: A Lifetime of Accomplishment, A Champion of Science Literacy," was held at the John F. Kennedy Center for the Performing Arts in Washington DC on May 20, 2013. It was announced at that event that NASA would create a new agency internship program in her name, and that an instrument on the International Space Station would bear her name. The EarthKAM is now known as the Sally Ride EarthKAM, and it still allows middle school students to take photographs from a digital camera mounted on the International Space Station.

That same year, 2013, Sally and fellow astronaut Neil Armstrong received the General James E. Hill Lifetime Space Achievement Award from the Space Foundation for their contributions to space exploration. Sally also was named a Stanford Engineering Hero by the school of engineering at her alma mater, a recognition given to scientists educated at Stanford who have aided humankind through engineering and science. In 2014, Sally was inducted into the Pioneer Hall of Fame by Women in Aviation International.

Sally continues to be honored to this day. America's newest oceanographic research vessel was named *R/V Sally Ride*. Christened by Secretary of the Navy Ray Mabus, the ship was launched in 2014 and is housed at Scripps Institution of Oceanography in La Jolla, California. Through Sally Ride Science at the University of California, San Diego, students and teachers can participate in ocean exploration and interact with scientists at sea in this vessel. Her dedication to education is also reflected in two schools, one in Texas and one in Maryland, that bear her name.

Although Sally scoffed at her own fame (having once commented, "I'm not historical material"), she did muse about her own legacy in 2006: "I would like to be remembered as someone who was not afraid to do what she wanted to do, and as someone who took risks along the way in order to achieve her goals." Steven Hawley, her former husband, may have stated what she accomplished the best:

"Sally Ride, the astronaut and the person, allowed many young girls across the world to believe they could achieve anything if they studied and worked hard. I think she would be pleased with that legacy."

There is little doubt that Sally Ride will ever be forgotten. After all, she has a spot on the moon named after her—the Sally K. Ride Impact Site. As her sister noted, "It's really cool to know that when you look up now at the moon, there's this little corner of the moon that's named after Sally."

That should inspire anyone.

Selected Sources

GENERAL REFERENCES

Women's Museum of California
2730 Historic Decatur Road, Suite 103
San Diego, CA 92106
http://womensmuseumca.org

National Women's History Project
730 Second Street #469
P.O. Box 469
Santa Rosa, CA 95402
http://www.nwhp.org

California Museum
Archives Plaza
1020 O Street
Sacramento, CA 95814
http://www.californiamuseum.org

National Women's History Museum
Administrative Offices
205 S. Whiting Street Suite 254
Alexandria, VA 22304
703-461-1920
http://www.nwhm.org

Hymowitz, Carol, and Michaele Weissman. 1978. *A History of Women in America: From Founding Mothers to Feminists.* New York: Bantam Books.

1. APOLINARIA LORENZANA

"Apolinaria Lorenzana." San Diego History Center. As found at: http://www.sandiegohistory.org/bio/lorenzana/lorenzana.htm.

"Apolinaria Lorenzana: The Blessed One." 2015. *Latino Rebels,* September 22. As found at: http://www.latinorebels.com.

Beebe, Rose Marie, and Robert M. Senkewicz, eds. 2015. *Testimonios: Early California through the Eyes of Women, 1815–1848.* Norman: University of Oklahoma Press.

Bouvier, Virginia M. 1993. Framing the Female Voice: The Bancroft Narratives of Apolinaria Lorenzana, Augustias de la Guerra Ord, and Eulalia Perez. In *Recovering the US Hispanic Literary Heritage* (Vol. 3), eds. Ramón A. Gutiérrez, Genaro M. Padilla, and Maria Herrera-Sobek. Houston, TX: Arte Publico Press.

Carter, Charles F. 1917. La Beata. In *Old Mission Stories of California.* London: Aeterna.

Cox, Elizabeth. 2003. *Southern California Miscellany.* San Luis Obispo, CA: McKenna Publishing Group.

"Latino Americans: Apolinaria Lorenzana." 2013. PBS Video, September 16. As found at: http://www.pbs.org/video/2365050307.

Lorenzana, Apolinaria. 1878. *Memorias de Dona Apolinaria Lorenzana, "Blessed" Made in Santa Barbara in March 1878 to Thomas Savage* (manuscript), University of California at Berkeley, Bancroft Library.

Mitchell, Pablo R. 2014. *History of Latinos: Exploring Diverse Roots.* Westport, CT: Greenwood.

Moynihan, Ruth B., Susan Armitage, and Christiane F. Dichamp, eds. 1998. *So Much to Be Done: Women Settlers on the Mining and Ranching Frontier* (2nd Ed.). Lincoln: University of Nebraska Press.

Ruiz, Vicki L., and Virginia S. Korrol, eds. 2006. *Latinas in the United States: A Historical Encyclopedia.* Bloomington: Indiana University Press.

Smith, Jeff. 2008. La Beata: The Life and Times of Apolinaria Lorenzana. *San Diego Reader*, June 25, July 2, and July 16.

2. BRIDGET "BIDDY" MASON

Biddy Mason Collection. University of California, Los Angeles, Research Library, Special Collection.

Brown, John. 1941. *Autobiography of John Brown.* Salt Lake City, UT: Stevens and Wallis, Inc. Also Journal Entries, 1848. As found at: http://heritage.uen.org.

Carpenter, Jane H., and Betye Saar. 2003. *Betye Saar.* Petaluma, CA: Pomegranate.

Colman, Penny. 2006. "Biddy Mason: Fierce Fighter." In *Adventurous Women: Eight True Stories About Women Who Made a Difference.* New York: Henry Holt and Company.

Crouch, Gregory. 1988. "Early Black Heroine of L.A. Finally Receives Her Due." *Los Angeles Times*, March 28.

Furbee, Mary R. 2002. *Outrageous Women of the American Frontier*. New York: Wiley.

Gavin, Camille. 2007. *Biddy Mason: A Place of Her Own*. Frederick, MD: America Star Books.

Gray, Dorothy. 1976. *Women of the West*. Lincoln: University of Nebraska Press.

Harris, Gloria G., and Hannah S. Cohen. 2012. *Women Trailblazers of California: Pioneers to the Present*. Charleston, SC: History Press.

Hayden, Dolores. 1989. "Biddy Mason's Los Angeles, 1856–1891." *California History* 68 (3): 86–99.

Katz, William L. 1995. *Black Women of the Old West*. New York: Atheneum.

Levy, Jo Ann. 1990. *They Saw the Elephant: Women in the California Gold Rush*. Hamden, CT: Archon Books.

Mason V. Smith. 1856. State of California, County of Los Angeles. First Judicial District State of California, County of Los Angeles. As found at: http://www.blackpast.org/primarywest/mason-v-smith-bridget-biddy-mason-case-1856.

Pool, Bob. 1991. "Proud Legacy." *Los Angeles Times*, July 31.

Smith, Jessie Carney, ed. 1992. *Notable Black American Women*. Farmington Hills, MI: Gale Research Inc.

Stanford, K. L. 2010. *African Americans in Los Angeles*. Charleston, SC: Arcadia Publishing.

Williams, Jean K. 2006. *Bridget "Biddy" Mason: From Slave to Businesswoman*. Mankato MN: Compass Point Books.

3. LUZENA STANLEY HUNT WILSON

"Awful Fire!" 1851. *Sacramento Transcript* 2 (118): March 13.

Chartier, JoAnn, and Chris Enss. 2000. *With Great Hope: Women of the California Gold Rush*. Guilford, CT: TwoDot/Falcon Publishing.

Collins, Gail. 2003. *America's Women: 400 Years of Dolls, Drudges, Helpmates, and Heroines*. New York: William Morrow.

Henry, Fern L. 2004. *My Checkered Life: Luzena Stanley Wilson in Early California*. Nevada City, CA: Carl Mautz Publishing.

Levy, Jo Ann. 1990. *They Saw the Elephant: Women in the California Gold Rush*. Hamden, CT: Archon Books.

Miller, Brandon M. 2013. *Women of the Frontier: 16 Tales of Trailblazing Homesteaders, Entrepreneurs, and Rabble-Rousers* (Women of Action). Chicago Review Press.

People and Events, The Gold Rush: Luzena Stanley Wilson. PBS. As found at: http://www.pbs.org.

The San Francisco Blue Book. 1888. Bancroft Company. As found at: https://archive.org/details/sanfranciscoblue1888sanf.

Wright, Correnah W. 2015. *Luzena Stanley Wilson, '49er: Her Memoirs as Taken Down by Her Daughter in 1881.* Firework Press. (Reprint of 1881 ed.)

4. NELLIE ELIZABETH POOLER CHAPMAN

Bean, Edwin F. 1867. *Bean's History and Directory of Nevada County, California: Containing a Complete History of the County, with Sketches of the Various Towns and Mining Camps . . . Also, Full Statistics of Mining and All Other Industrial Resources.* Nevada: Daily Gazette Book and Job Office. E-book.

Board of Certifications Doctors and Dentists 1876–1928. Archived at the Doris Foley Library for Historical Research, 211 N. Pine Street, Nevada City, CA, 95959.

California GenWeb for Nevada County. *Surname Index to Corporations.* As found at: http://www.cagenweb.com/nevada/data/nccorp_surnames_C-D.html. Also Original Nevada City Lot owners–1869. As found at: http://www.cagenweb.com/nevada/nclots/nclots-7.html.

Chapman, Robert M. 1974. "Passed to the Great Beyond: Dr. Allen Chapman Joins the Silent Majority." *Sutter-Yuba Digger Digest* I (3). As found at: http://www.yubaroots.com/nuggets/diggers-v1-3.pdf.

Chartier, Joann, and Chris Enss. 2000. *With Great Hope: Women of the California Gold Rush.* Guilford, CT: TwoDot/Falcon Publishing.

Collins, Gail. 2003. *America's Women: 400 Years of Dolls, Drudges, Helpmates, and Heroines.* New York: William Morrow.

Enss, Chris. 2006. *The Doctor Wore Petticoats: Women Physicians of the Old West.* Guilford, CT: TwoDot.

Enss, Chris. 2007. *Tales Behind the Tombstones: The Deaths and Burials of the Old West's Most Nefarious Outlaws, Notorious Women, and Celebrated Lawmen.* Guilford, CT: TwoDot.

Guinn, James M. 1906. *History of the State of California and Biographical Record of the Sierras: A Historical Story of the State's Marvelous Growth from Its Earliest Settlement to the Present Time.* Chicago: Chapman Publishing Company.

Harris, Gloria G., and Hannah S. Cohen 2012. *Women Trailblazers of California: Pioneers to the Present.* Charleston, SC: History Press.

Kaiser Family Foundation. 2016. "Professionally Active Dentists by Gender." As found at: http://kff.org/other/state-indicator/total-dentists-by-gender/.

Kiley, Bill. 1990. "A 'Practicing' Woman Dentist, the First in the West." *Sierra Heritage* (November-December): 57–61.

Mann, Ralph. 1982. *After the Gold Rush: Society in Grass Valley and Nevada City, California, 1849–1870.* Redwood City, CA: Stanford University Press.

"Obituary: Dr. Nellie E. Chapman." 1906. *Pacific Dental Gazette* 14: 282.

Van der Pas, Peter W. 1990. "The Chapman Family of Nevada City." *Nevada County Historical Society Bulletin* 44 (4): 26–28.

Weisner, Susan. 2011. "Allen Chapman and Nellie Pooler Chapman–Bringing Dentistry to Nevada City." *Greater Cement Hill Neighborhood Association Newsletter*, Nevada City, CA. As found at: http://www.gchna.com/wp-content/uploads/2010/08/Summer-2011.pdf.

5. TOBY "WINEMA" RIDDLE

Bales, Rebecca. 2005. "Winema and the Modoc War: One Woman's Struggle for Peace." *Prologue Magazine* 37 (1).

Brown, Frederick L. 2011. *The Center of the World, The Edge of the World: A History of Lava Beds National Monument.* National Park Service.

Chartier, Jo Ann, and Chris Enss. 2004. *She Wore a Yellow Ribbon: Women Soldiers and Patriots of the Western Frontier.* Guilford, CT: TwoDot.

Cothran, Boyd. 2014. *Remembering the Modoc War: Redemptive Violence and the Making of American Innocence.* Chapel Hill, NC: University of North Carolina Press. Taken from *Marketplaces of Remembering: Violence, Colonialism, and American Innocence in the Making of the Modoc War*, Dissertation (2012), University of Minnesota.

"The Death of Canby; The End of Poor Lo." 1873. *Memphis Daily Appeal.* April 13. As found at: http://chroniclingamerica.loc.gov.

Gray-Kanatiiosh, Barbara A. 2007. *Modoc.* Minneapolis, MN: Abdo Pub.

Harris, Gloria G., and Hannah S. Cohen. 2012. *Women Trailblazers of California: Pioneers to the Present.* Charleston, SC: History Press.

Lava Beds National Park. *A Brief History of the Modoc War.* National Park Service. As found at: http://www.nps.gov/labe/planyourvisit.

"Modoc Indian Basket Returned." 1954. *Reno Evening Gazette,* December 7.

PBS. 2011. "Modoc Basket." *History Detectives* Episode 809. As found at http://www.pbs.org/opb/historydetectives/investigation/modoc-basket.

Quinn, Arthur. 1997. *Hell With the Fire Out: A History of the Modoc War.* London: Faber and Faber, Inc.

Riddle, Jeff C. 1914. *Indian History of the Modoc War.* Mechanicsburg, PA: Stackpole Books.

"The Story of Wi-Ne-Ma: She Risked Her Life to Avert War and Prevent Murder." 1895. *New York Times,* October 27.

"Toby Riddle." No date. *New World Encyclopedia.* As found at: http://www.new-worldencyclopedia.org.

Thompson, Erwin N. 1971. *Modoc War: Its Military History and Topography.* Kernersville, NC: Argus Books.

White, Julia. No Date. "Kaitchkona Winema–Modoc." As found at: http://www.powersource.com/gallery/womansp/winema.html.

6. ELVIRA VIRGINIA MUGARRIETA

"Babe Bean, the Mysterious Ark-Dweller." 1897. Stockton *Evening Mail,* October 9.

Beam, B. 1900. "My Life as a Soldier." *San Francisco Examiner,* October 21.

"Death of Woman Shows She Lived as Man 40 Years." 1936. *Woodville Republican,* December 26.

Boag, Peter. 2012. *Re-dressing America's Frontier Past.* Oakland, CA: University of California Press.

California, State Hospital Records, 1856–1923 for Elvira Mugarrieta. Stockton State Hospital. Commitment Registers, Vol. 9–10. 1886–1894.

"Death Discloses Woman had Posed as Man for 38 Years." 1936. *Milwaukee Journal,* September 21.

"Girl Dressed in Men's Togs Held in German Plot." *1917. Chicago Tribune,* December 30.

"Latinas in History." 2008. Mugarrieta, Elvira Virginia (Babe Bean, Jack Bee Garland) (1869–1936). As found at http://depthome.brooklyn.cuny.edu/latinashistory/mugaretaelviravirginia1.html.

"Little Miss Adventure." 1897. Stockton *Evening Mail,* August 23.

San Francisco Lesbian and Gay History Project. 1989. She Even Chewed Tobacco: A Pictorial Narrative of Passing Women in America. In *Hidden from History: Reclaiming the Gay and Lesbian Past,* eds. Martin Duberman and others. New York: NAL Books.

Skidmore, Emily E. 2011. *Exceptional Queerness: Defining the Boundaries of US Citizenship, 1876–1936.* Doctoral dissertation, University of Illinois at Urbana-Champaign.

Stephens, Autumn. 1992. *Wild Women: Crusaders, Curmudgeons, and Completely Corsetless Ladies in the Otherwise Virtuous Victorian Era.* Newburyport, MA: Conari Press.

Stryker, Susan, and Stephen Whittle. 2006. *The Transgender Studies Reader.* New York: Taylor and Francis.

Sullivan, Louis. 1990. *From Female to Male: The Life of Jack Bee Garland.* New York: Alyson Books.

Sullivan, Louis G. 1987. Elvira Mugarrieta Alias Jack Bee Garland or in Stockton, Babe Bean. *San Joaquin Historian* 1 (3): 1–10.

7. JULIA MORGAN

Alter, Judy. 1999. *Extraordinary Women of the American West.* Chicago: Children's Press.

Boutelle, Sara Holmes. 1988. *Julia Morgan, Architect.* New York: Abbeville Press.

Craven, Jackie. *Julia Morgan, Designer of Hearst Castle (1872–1957).* As found at: http://architecture.about.com/od/greatarchitects/p/juliamorgan.htm.

Harris, Gloria G., and Hannah S. Cohen. 2012. *Women Trailblazers of California: Pioneers to the Present.* Charleston, SC: History Press.

Jacobs, Karrie. 2013. "Julia Morgan Posthumously Awarded the AIA 2014 Gold Medal." *Architect Magazine*, December 12. As found at: http://www.architectmagazine.com/awards.

James, Cary. 1990. *Julia Morgan, Architect.* New York: Chelsea House Publications.

"Julia Morgan: An Online Exhibition." Robert E. Kennedy Library, California Polytechnic State University. As found at: http://lib.calpoly.edu.

Kastner, Victoria. 2009. *Hearst's San Simeon: The Gardens and the Land.* New York: Harry N. Abrams.

Mannis, Celeste. 2006. *Julia Morgan Built a Castle.* New York: Viking Juvenile.

Wadsworth, Ginger. 1990. *Julia Morgan, Architect of Dreams.* Minneapolis, MN: Lerner Publications.

Wilson, Mark. 2012. *Julia Morgan: Architect of Beauty.* Layton, UT: Gibbs Smith.

8. TAREA HALL PITTMAN

Brillant, Mark. 2012. *The Color of America Has Changed: How Racial Diversity Shaped Civil Rights Reform in California, 1941–1978.* Oxford University Press.

Broussard, Albert S. 1993. *Black San Francisco: The Struggle for Racial Equality in the West, 1900–1954.* Lawrence, KS: University Press of Kansas.

Cavin, Aaron I. 2012. *The Borders of Citizenship: The Politics of Race and Metropolitan Space in Silicon Valley.* Doctoral dissertation, University of Michigan.

Crowe, Daniel E. 2000. *Prophets of Rage: The Black Freedom Struggle in San Francisco, 1945–1969.* New York: Routledge.

Finkelman, Paul, ed. 2009. *Encyclopedia of African American History, 1896 to the Present: From the Age of Segregation to the Twenty-First Century.* Oxford University Press.

Fleming, Thomas C. "The National Negro Congress of 1936." *The Columbus Free Press,* September 22, 1999. As found at: http://freepress.org.

Fousekis, Natalie. 2006. "Pittman, Tarea Hall (1903–1991)." In *Encyclopedia of Immigration and Migration in the American West* (Vol. 2), eds. Gordon M. Bakken and Alexandra Kindell, 541–45. Thousand Oaks, CA: Sage Publications.

Lemke-Santangelo, Gretchen. 1996. *Abiding Courage: African American Migrant Women and the East Bay Community.* Chapel Hill: University of North Carolina Press.

Oakland Museum of California. "World War II Homefront Era: 1940s: Women Replace Men in the Workforce." As found at: http://picturethis. museumca.org/timeline/world-war-ii-homefront-era-1940s/women-labor/ info.

Pittman, Tarea H. November 20, 1956. *Letter to Annie L. Barnett.* Carton 7, NAACP West Coast Regional Papers. Berkeley, CA: Bancroft Library, University of California.

Pittman, Tarea H., and Joyce A. Henderson. 1974. *Tarea Hall Pittman, NAACP Official and Civil Rights Worker: An Interview.* Earl Warren Oral History Project. Berkeley, CA: Bancroft Library, University of California.

Rex, Kyle. "Pittman, Tarea Hall (1903–1991)." As found at: http://www. blackpast.org.

Scherr, Judith. 2015. "Berkeley residents call for renaming library." *Times-Herald News,* February 18.

De Graaf, Lawrence B., Kevin Mulroy, and Quintard Taylor, eds. *2001. Seeking El Dorado: African Americans in California.* Los Angeles: Autry Museum of Western Heritage.

"Tarea H. Pittman, Human Rights Worker: Obituary." 1991. *San Francisco Chronicle,* August 3.

Taylor, Quintard, and Shirley Ann W. Moore, eds. 2003. *African American Women Confront the West: 1600–2000.* Norman: University of Oklahoma Press.

"World War II Shipbuilding in the San Francisco Bay Area." National Park Service. As found at: http://www.nps.gov/nr/travel/wwiibayarea/ shipbuilding.HTM.

9. YOSHIKO UCHIDA

Chang, Catherine E. Studier. 1984. "Profile: Yoshiko Uchida." *Language Arts* 61 (2): 189–94.

Collins, Gail. 2003. *America's Women: 400 Years of Dolls, Drudges, Helpmates, and Heroines.* New York: William Morrow.

Glencoe McGraw-Hill. "Meet Yoshiko Uchida." Study Guide for *Picture Bride* by Yoshiko Uchida. As found at: http://www.glencoe.com.

"Japanese Americans during WWII: Relocation & Internment: Personal Justice Denied." National Archives. As found at: http://www.archives.gov/research/japanese-americans/justice-denied.

Niiya, Brian. "Yoshiko Uchida." In *Densho Encyclopedia.* As found at: http://encyclopedia.densho.org.

Norton, Donna E. 2011. *Through the Eyes of a Child: An Introduction to Children's Literature* (8th ed.). New York: Pearson.

Uchida, Yoshiko. 1971. *Journey to Topaz.* New York: Scribner.

Uchida, Yoshiko. 1972. *Samurai of Gold Hill.* New York: Charles Scribner's Sons.

Uchida, Yoshiko. 1978. *Journey Home.* New York: Atheneum.

Uchida, Yoshiko. 1982. *Desert Exile: The Uprooting of an American Family.* Seattle: University of Washington Press.

Uchida, Yoshiko 1991. *The Invisible Thread: An Autobiography.* New York: Julian Messner.

"Yoshiko Uchida, 70, A Children's Author: Obituary." 1992. *New York Times* June 24. As found at: http://www.nytimes.com.

Yoshiko Uchida papers, 1903–1994. Berkeley, CA: Bancroft Library, University of California.

10. ROSE ANN VUICH

Collins, Gail. 2009. *When Everything Changed: The Amazing Journey of American Women from 1960 to the Present.* New York: Little, Brown and Company.

Dooley, Calvin M. 2001. "A Tribute to Rose Ann Vuich." *CapitolWords* 147 (115): E1604–E1605.

"First female state senator Vuich Dies at Age 74." 2001. *Napa Valley Register,* September 1.

Ingram, Carl. 1988. "Once-Praised Vuich Now Rated Too Independent for Governor." *Los Angeles Times,* April 5. As found at: https://articles.latimes.com/.

McHale, Terry. "Rose Ann Vuich." *Capitol Morning Report,* February 4, 2002.

Paddock, Richard, and Paul Jacobs. 1990. "US Prosecutors Smeared Montoya, Lawyer Tells Jury." *Los Angeles Times,* January 30.

Reingold, Beth. 2000. *Representing Women: Sex, Gender, and Legislative Behavior in Arizona and California.* Chapel Hill: University of North Carolina Press.

Sproul, Kate. 1999. *Women and Equality: A California Review of Women's Equity Issues in Civil Rights, Education and the Workplace*. California Senate Office of Research. Dedication. As found at: https://books.google.com/books.

"Vuich Raps Bid to Limit Users of Federal Water." 1977. *Bakersfield Californian*, October 17.

Weatherford, Doris. 2012. *Women in American Politics: History and Milestones*. Washington, DC: CQ Press.

"Women, Republicans Fared Poorly in Legislature." 1976. *San Bernardino County Sun*, November 4.

Woo, Elaine. 2001. "Obituary: Rose Ann Vuich; First Woman in the State Senate." *Los Angeles Times*, September 1.

11. SHIRLEY TEMPLE BLACK

Black, Shirley T. 1988. *Child Star: An Autobiography*. New York: McGraw-Hill.

Blashfield, Jean F. 2000. *Shirley Temple Black: Actor and Diplomat*. New York: Ferguson.

Edwards, Anne. 1988. *Shirley Temple: American Princess*. New York: William Morrow.

Harmetz, Alijean. 2014. "Shirley Temple Black, Hollywood's Biggest Little Star, Dies at 85." *The New York Times*, February 11. As found at: http://www.nytimes.com.

Kasson, John F. 2014. *The Little Girl Who Fought the Great Depression: Shirley Temple and 1930s America*. New York: W. W. Norton and Company.

Miklowitz, Gloria D. 2004. *Shirley Temple Black*. Carlsbad, CA: Dominie Elementary.

The Official Shirley Temple Website. http://www.shirleytemple.com.

Roosevelt, Eleanor. July 11, 1938. *My Day*. As found at: http://www.gwu.edu/~erpapers/myday/displaydoc.cfm?_y=1938&_f=md055002.

12. DOLORES HUERTA

Doak, Robin S. 2008. *Dolores Huerta: Labor Leader and Civil Rights Activist*. Mankato, MN: Compass Point Books.

"Dolores Huerta: Co-Founder, United Farm Workers, San Joaquin Delta College." California Community Colleges Chancellor's Office. As found at: http://californiacommunitycolleges.cccco.edu/Newsroom/Notable Alumni/DoloresHuerta.aspx.

"Dolores Huerta Remembers Grape Boycott on 50th Anniversary of March to Sacramento." 2016. *Fox Latino News*, March 17.

Foundation, Dolores Huerta. "Dolores Huerta Biography: The Feminist Seed Is Planted." As found at: http://www.doloreshuerta.org/dolores-huerta.

Garcia, Mario T., ed. 2008. *A Dolores Huerta Reader*. Albuquerque: University of New Mexico Press.

Garza, Hedda. 2001. *Latinas: Hispanic Women in the United States*. Albuquerque: University of New Mexico Press.

Gillis, Jennifer B. 2005. *American Lives: Dolores Huerta*. New York: Heinemann.

Harris, Gloria G., and Hannah S. Cohen. 2012. *Women Trailblazers of California: Pioneers to the Present*. Charleston, SC: History Press.

Hightower-Langston, Donna. 2002. *A to Z of American Women Leaders and Activists*. New York: Infobase Publishing.

Miller, Debra A. 2006. *Dolores Huerta: Labor Leader*. Farmington Hills, MI: Thomson Gale/Lucent Books.

Rose, Margaret. 1993. "Dolores Huerta: Labor Leader, Social Activist." In *Notable Hispanic Women*, eds. Diane Telgen and Jim Kemp. Farmington Hills, MI: Gale Publishing.

Schatz, Kate. 2015. *Rad American Women A-Z*. San Francisco: City Lights Books.

Warren, Sarah. 2012. *Dolores Huerta: A Hero to Migrant Workers*. Tarrytown, NY: Marshall Cavendish Children.

Worth, Richard. 2007. *Dolores Huerta*. New York: Chelsea House.

13. SALLY RIDE

Bergin, Chris, and Chris Gebhardt. 2012. "The Passing of Sally Ride: The Legacy of a True Shuttle Pioneer." NASASpaceflight.com, July 24.

"Dr. Sally Ride." As found at: http://starchild.gsfc.nasa.gov/docs/StarChild/whos_who_level2/ride.html

Macy, Sue. 2014. *Sally Ride: Life on a Mission*. New York: Aladdin.

Matten, Joanne. 2009. *Sally Ride, Astronaut*. New York: Infobase Publishing.

Nettleton, Pamela H. 2003. *Sally Ride: Astronaut, Scientist, Teacher*. Mankato, MN: Picture Window Books.

Nichols, Catherine. 2005. *Sally Ride*. New York: Scholastic.

Piercey, Judy, and Jennifer Davies. 2015. "Sally Ride Science Launches at UC San Diego." *UC San Diego News Center*, October 22. As found at: http://ucsdnews.ucsd.edu.

Ride, Sally, and Susan Okie. 1986. *To Space and Back*. NY: Lothrop, Lee and Shepard.

Stine, Megan. 2013. *Who Was Sally Ride?* New York: Grosset & Dunlap.

Wall, Mike. 2012. "Moon Probes' Crash Site Named After Sally Ride." Space.com, December 17. As found at: http://www.space.com.

Index

KAY MOORE was born and raised in Maryland where she was surrounded by sites of importance from many historical events. Exploring these turned her into an incorrigible history buff at an early age with a special interest in the lives of women and children. Moving to California to become an elementary school teacher, and later a university educator, she lived for many years in Placerville (originally called "Hangtown," but the name was changed to reflect less violent placer mining). Upon retirement from California State University, Sacramento, Kay moved to Las Vegas where she and her grandchildren have started exploring the historical sites of Nevada. She is the author of several nonfiction juvenile books, including the award-winning *The Great Bicycle Experiment: The Army's Historic Black Bicycle Corps, 1896–97.*

Written for ages 12 and up, the Bold Women series features women who pushed through adversity to carve their own paths and achieve their personal dreams. Their stories prove what women can accomplish when they dare to be BOLD.

OTHER BOOKS AVAILABLE IN THIS SERIES

Bold Women in Alaska History

Bold Women in Colorado History

Bold Women in Indiana History

Bold Women in Michigan History

Bold Women in Montana History

Bold Women in Texas History

MP **Mountain Press**
PUBLISHING COMPANY

P.O. Box 2399 • Missoula, MT 59806 • 406-728-1900
800-234-5308 • info@mtnpress.com
www.mountain-press.com